PURE ANIMATION

PURE ANIMATION

Steps to Creation with 57 Cutting-Edge Animators

Spencer Drate
Judith Salavetz

Foreword by
J.J. Sedelmaier

MERRELL
LONDON · NEW YORK

CONTENTS

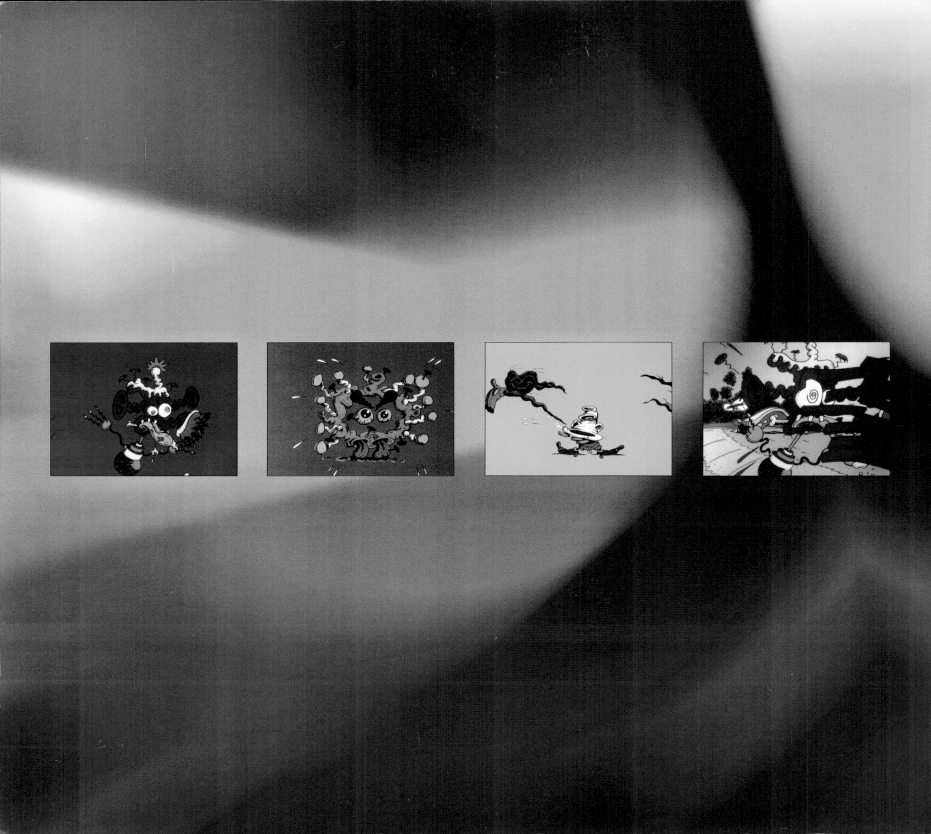

FOREWORD

In 2006, we celebrated the centennial of J. Stuart Blackton's film *Humorous Phases of Funny Faces*, the cartoon that is regarded as being the first American animated film. It seems to me that it's only in the past ten to fifteen years, however, that animation's potential to appeal to all ages has been recognized.

Walt Disney's success in the medium was double-edged. It catapulted the craft into a realm of high visibility and popular culture, and brought it worldwide popular approval, but its influence was overwhelming. Only recently has animation been able to step out of Disney's shadow to surprise and delight different audiences in unexpected ways.

How did we get where we are today? A great deal of change in the craft— in how it's used and how it's perceived—is linked to the development of computer technology. In fact, I think computer technology, like the growth of television in the 1950s, has been one of the most important influences on the animation industry since its beginning. Computer animation (also known as 3D, or CGI: Computer Generated Imagery) has not only revolutionized the art with its enthralling visuals of hyper-real quality, but has also opened people's eyes to the strengths and weaknesses of the different techniques. Such styles as stop-motion, pixilation, and good old traditional animation (2D, cel, or cartoon), are being understood and embraced for their unique production qualities.

When computer animation hit the screen in the mid-1990s with such films as Disney's *Toy Story*, reports of the demise of traditional animation began to proliferate. This shortsighted and dollar-driven reaction is being proved wrong, however. As a glut of CGI projects are released to cash in on the current trend, audiences and critics are beginning to question the technique's versatility. CGI visuals have a formulaic and somewhat cold look, and the more closely they mimic reality, the further they edge toward the live-action realm, instead of relying on an animator's interpretation of reality. Why use animation if all you're going to do is imitate live action?

Audiences and critics who question the over-use of CGI are also re-evaluating the warmth and human qualities inherent in such techniques as 2D and stop-motion—the unique charm that results from use of the human hand. What was once considered to be a deficiency or imperfection is now valued; we're beginning to realize that there's room for more than one style in this business.

The popularity of 2D effects also owes something to nostalgia. CGI is the visual language of choice for today's kids, thanks to everything from motion pictures to gaming, but the kids of the 1950s through the 1970s speak the 2D dialect. They took in everything from classic theatrical cartoon shorts to the embarrassingly inadequate material produced for Saturday-morning television, and they have brought their cartoon baggage with them into adulthood. MTV networks—and later Nickelodeon—were perceptive enough in the early 1980s to seize on this and attract audiences by producing animated network IDs. Talented studios and individuals were contracted to create these ten- to fifteen-

second interstitials in an array of styles. Each one had to highlight the distinctive MTV logo in a clever, edgy, or fun way. This helped turn people's perception of animation on its head: what had been a user-friendly technique aimed primarily at kids now became a poke in the eye for adolescents and adults.

Once MTV's success had taken hold, the advertising community started to apply the same approaches to animated television ads. This led to the creation of Matt Groening's *The Simpsons*, Nickelodeon and John Kricfalusi's *Ren & Stimpy*, Mike Judge's *Beavis and Butt-Head*, the Saturday TV Funhouse cartoons for *Saturday Night Live*, and Trey Parker and Matt Stone's *South Park*. All these visually traditional cartoon styles have an updated sensibility and are designed to appeal not just to children but to adults as well. They all use the 2D, hands-on, human touch, which disarms the viewer, thereby getting the message across with greater effect. It's not surprising that this climate also produced a twenty-four-hour Cartoon Network.

Canadian animator Richard Williams deserves enormous credit for helping to resurrect the traditional animated cartoon. A lover of the classic Hollywood cartoons and an admirer of their creators, Williams demanded the highest standards in his work for television and motion pictures. His dedication to quality was exceptional—especially during the late 1960s and early 1970s in the United States—and put less committed studios to shame. He won a great deal of work from the United States, persuading even the advertising agencies on Madison Avenue to move to his London studio. Pulling such journeyman animators as Art Babbitt out of retirement to teach his artists classic techniques, Williams re-energized a craft that was on the verge of creative collapse. He is also known for animating the early *Pink Panther* movie titles, for winning an Academy Award for his *Christmas Carol* short, and for being animation director on *Who Framed Roger Rabbit*. Now Williams teaches seminars to packed audiences.

Last, I want to mention independent animators—the most scandalously underrated contributors to animation's heritage. Few people realize what such filmmakers as Priit Pärn, George Griffin, and Peter Faldes have done for the medium. Although some people may have heard of the influential stop-motion animators Brothers Quay, without the contributions of the independent animator there would be no MTV interstitials, no fresh ideas and attitudes for the mainstream media to use as inspiration. Such visionaries as these paved the way for the big studios, the networks, and Madison Avenue.

Now, let's talk anime.

J. J. Sedelmaier
President and Creative Director, J. Sedelmaier Productions

J. J. Sedelmaier
PRODUCTIONS, INC.

PREFACE

Animation is about people. Bugs Bunny isn't just a cartoon rabbit; he's an individual in his own right, with feelings, attitudes, and desires. The same goes for the myriad bouncing bottle caps, spirited cars, and assertive toys seen in animated commercials and feature films: they are inanimate initially, but the second they move, they take on a personality. So do all those abstract shapes and effects—snow, fire, smoke—that twist and undulate, expressing human urges and passions. This vitality is what brings audiences to animation; it inspires students to seek instruction, and teachers and practitioners to teach—all of them seduced by the art's charm and excitement.

Good animators learn early on that style and technique are important, but the emotional aspect of their stories and designs—the people part—is where the real strength lies. For fifty years, this has been the primary approach to teaching animation at the School of Visual Arts in New York. The instructors, all working artists, leave their own desks to encourage enthusiastic young people in a range of classes, from storyboard creation to character animation and design-inspired computer graphics. The fundamental principles are that animation reflects human feelings through motion art, and that this human stamp is what holds the viewers' attention. A good thing, too, since virtually every kind of art vies for attention on a screen somewhere these days. Animation offers a variety of visual concepts not usually associated with live-action film: it opens up both the artists' and the audience's imaginations. Students soon realize that lines and shapes that move excite people.

Animation reflects what's happening in the world. Everyday events filter through into animators' work, as do the shifting influences of inventions, sport, wars, politics, art, show business, and personal life. They are reflected in such incarnations as *South Park*, *Rugrats*, and *The Simpsons*; in feature films, TV commercials, public-service spots, and educational videos; and in a hundred thousand websites. Further inspiration lies in the ingenious experiments of Scottish-born animation pioneer Norman McLaren, the warm reflections of John Hubley (who developed the character of Mr. Magoo, among numerous others), the delicate imagery of the Russian filmmaker Yuri Norstein, and the stylized enthusiasm of Tim Burton's *Corpse Bride* and Brad Bird's *The Incredibles*. Students have much to see and absorb while developing their own personal styles.

Of course, dedicated animators should be constantly on their guard to avoid clichés, no matter how strong their admiration of popular styles or how insistent the demands of a commercially competitive field. The ever-expanding technology of computers can encourage and facilitate new ways of expression, but it can also make imitation of others' achievements an easy option.

Pure Animation offers inspiring works from all aspects of the craft for readers to peruse, admire, and emulate; but let's hope it will also embolden and—yes—animate some of us to seek new heights of creation in this uniquely moving medium.

Howard Beckerman and **Reeves Lehman**

Howard Beckerman *is an animation artist, animation historian, animation-restoration artist, and teacher at the School of Visual Arts, New York.*

Reeves Lehman *is Chairman of the Film/Video/Animation Department at the School of Visual Arts, New York.*

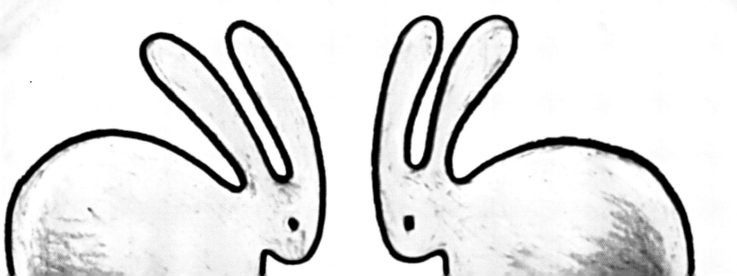

INTRODUCTION

As children, we experienced the delight of cartoons; as adults, we were exhilarated by a medium coming of age; and as working professionals, we marvel as the genre continues its dazzling evolution. We have endeavored to share this enjoyment by compiling and designing a book that will entertain and educate present and future generations.

Of course, there have been books on animation before, but this one is different. We have the award-winners and the well-established names, but we've also included a few newcomers who are just starting to make a name for themselves. Although our contributors all stand at the forefront of this creative medium, many have never before been published in book form.

While certain animation companies receive wide coverage, there are many others of at least equal creative accomplishment that deserve exposure. We were guided in our choice of contributors by such experts as J.J. Sedelmaier, founder, president, and creative director of J.J. Sedelmaier Productions; Nancy Phelps, member of the International Board of the International Animated Film Association; David Levy, president of the International Animation Film Society; and Chris Robinson, director of the Ottawa International Animation Festival.

This book encompasses a wide spectrum of international styles, some of which may be unfamiliar—though complementary—to those in the American market. The three major styles represented are: 2D/traditional, the exponents of which include Foreign Office, Andreas Hykade, J.J. Sedelmaier Productions, and Chaotic Unicorn; 3D, represented, among others, by Studio aka, Addikt, and Alexandre Siqueira; and modeling/stop-motion, as produced, for example, by Odeon and Arthur Suydam.

We wanted to create a book that spoke to students of animation as well as to those with more experience. We made sure we included enough visual-sequencing frames from which anyone could learn, as well as explanatory technical jargon and hands-on practical information. We hope you will enjoy the results.

Cue the music!

Spencer Drate and **Judith Salavetz**

5-X-B
USA
TITLE: LUMBERJACK GAMES
CLIENT: ECKO UNLIMITED
FORMAT: IN-STORE PROMO VIDEO

PROFILE

In 2004, 5-x-b was founded by creative directors/animators Max Matzenbacher and Austin Blasingame, and designer/producer Alana Blasingame. It has generated standout graphics for such diverse clients as IFC, BET, AMC, and ABC. The company prides itself on its adaptability, on creating unique visual pieces, and on continually exceeding expectations and driving creative standards upward. In addition to motion graphics, 5-x-b produces modern art, fashion, and cutting-edge design.

STEPS TO CREATION

Ecko had a nebulous idea for a segment of its soon-to-be-launched Ecko TV project: a pair of rhino toys that the 5-x-b team named Squidlet and G-bus. A few simple scripts were developed that described the shots and the elements needed for each, and Ecko chose the lumberjack games concept.

A storyboard was drawn up to establish the compositions, visible props, and character motion. Meanwhile, the 3D props were built: chainsaws, axes, logs, and so on. The rhinos were shot

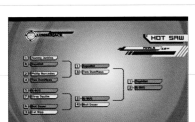

using stop-motion, and a rough animatic integrated the basic scene setups with the rhino footage. The team then rendered and textured the 3D elements and composited the woodchip particles, the rhino footage, and matte paintings of the crowd. The final step was to add the soundtrack: a voice-over for commentary, and other background sounds that reflected the Ecko spin on a sports-center broadcast.

TOOLS
Adobe After Effects, Apple Final Cut Pro, Autodesk Maya

CREDITS
Director: Austin Blasingame
Producer: Alana Blasingame
Illustration: Jason Brubaker
Animation: Brian Castleforte
Compositing: Max Matzenbacher

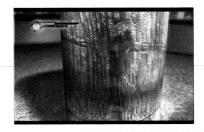
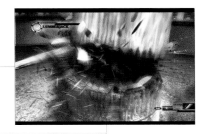

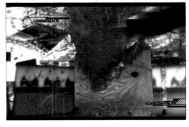

5-X-B
TITLE: WICK'D
CLIENT: BET J
FORMAT: TITLE SEQUENCE

STEPS TO CREATION

For this opener for the Wick'd Caribbean music video show, the BET J cable network pulled tracks from its files and passed them on to 5-x-b. Having grown up with the deep-rooted reggae of such artists as Jimmy Cliff, Peter Tosh, and Bob Marley, the team found that the creative direction of this piece came right from the music. They said they just let themselves go and had tons of fun with it, and created what they felt to be a rich Caribbean island vibe. They wanted the piece to have an upbeat, dreamy quality that accented the rhythm of island music.

The first phase of the project was spent breaking down the various illustrations and giving the animations a simple rhythmic quality. The rest of the process involved integrating 2D and 3D elements spatially. Elements were constantly being passed around, going from 2D to 3D space and back. The goal was to try to convey a sense of "Utopian chill."

TOOLS
Adobe After Effects, Maxon Cinema 4D

CREDITS
Director: Austin Blasingame
Producer: Alana Blasingame
Animation: Andrew Hoovler, Marisol Baltierra
Compositing: Max Matzenbacher

180 AMSTERDAM
THE NETHERLANDS
TITLE: MODULAR MAN
CLIENT: ADIDAS INTERNATIONAL
FORMAT: WEB COMMERCIAL

PROFILE

International creative agency 180 Amsterdam has offices in Amsterdam and Los Angeles, and employs over one hundred people from more than twenty countries. 180's client roster includes Sony Consumer Electronics, Motorola, Opel (General Motors Europe), Amstel Beer, Glenfiddich, Omega Watches, Dr Pepper, and Amnesty International.

STEPS TO CREATION

180 Amsterdam was commissioned to make an ad for the modular Adidas Tunit football boot—the boot that allows user customization for a variety of playing surfaces. Since the concept was "Assemble Your Own Boot," the idea evolved of assembling modular players, showing their bodies separating and rebuilding.

At that point, 180 Amsterdam contacted New York-based CGI VFX/animation studio 1st Ave Machine. The two companies worked together

to develop the character designs and to conceptualize how the sections would look and connect, based on human muscle groups. The scripts were written by 180 Amsterdam. The agency also filmed the players in London in an extensive motion-capture session. Then the 1st Ave Machine gang started putting things together from the data.

1st Ave Machine used 3D Studio Max to create the 3D modular players. Each player was composed of some 400 different pieces. Executive producer Serge Patzak explained: "We had to figure out exactly how each would break apart, what the pieces would be composed of, how they would connect with the boot, and a whole mess of other considerations. We worked with 180 Amsterdam on this idea of modularity, the notion that these pieces were in some sense interchangeable, yet uniquely powerful in each modular construct."

When the 180 Amsterdam team saw the modular men, they had this idea that their creators must have been working to the accompaniment of classical music, and they decided to use Beethoven's *Moonlight Sonata* in the ad.

In their pursuit of a precise, hyper-real look, 1st Ave Machine and 180 Amsterdam took advantage of another Adidas commercial shoot to get complete head scans of each of the players. The campaign has since been expanded to include a series of animated spots featuring all the main players. In addition, the characters will be used in online video games and will be featured on the large screens at the 2010 World Cup.

TOOLS
Autodesk 3D Studio Max, Autodesk V-Ray

CREDITS
Director: Andy Fackrell
Producers: Serge Patzak, Cedric Gairard, Peter Cline, Kate Morrison
Animation: Arvind Palem
Music Composition: Ludwig van Beethoven

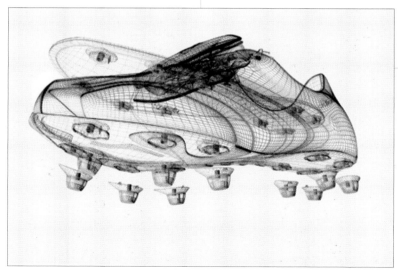

ABSOLUTE POST PRODUCTION
UK
TITLE: MAYFLY
CLIENT: VODAFONE
FORMAT: TV + FILM COMMERCIAL

PROFILE

Absolute Post Production was set up in 2004 by one of the world's leading Flame talents, David Smith. With three full-time Flame suites running 24/7, Absolute specializes in providing high-level visual effects for TV commercials and promos. Its client list includes BBH, AMV.BBDO, and Mother; such brands as Mercedes-Benz, Honda, and Levi's; such production companies as Gorgeous, @Radical.media, and HSI; and such directors as Peter Thwaites, Paul Street, and David LaChapelle.

STEPS TO CREATION

This ad for Vodafone, coordinated by BBH, concentrates on the fun that can be had with Vodafone's various chat, romance, gaming, and video services. This uplifting spot encourages viewers to embrace life like the humble mayfly, which, although it has only one day to live, knows how to live life to the max. Passion Pictures created the mayfly in CGI, and Absolute's Phil Oldham led the complex compositing.

The action is set in a lush Thai jungle, and the scene opens with the birth of the mayfly. It soars into the sky. As the mayfly

descends, the fun begins. It uses leaves as slides and kayaks, plays leaf tennis over a spider's web, juggles with flower petals, and then finally—in the winter of its short life—the mayfly finds true love.

Gradually, Passion's extremely realistic mayfly gains more character animation as the spot progresses from documentary style to Disney style. When the animation was supplied to Absolute, Oldham began the tricky process of compositing. Owing to the use of macrophotography, the mayfly's depth of field tended to be extreme, so Oldham had to find the correct balance between sharpness and softness.

Oldham was also charged with introducing Vodafone's brand color red into the edit. His solution was to go to London's well-known Berwick Street Market to buy brightly colored flowers, which he then photographed on Absolute's roof terrace and composited into the jungle scenes. Flame was then used to re-grade some initial stock footage scenes and composite all the watery mayfly reflections. The team used stock footage and Internet-sourced material to create a matte painting for some of the panoramic jungle shots.

TOOLS
Autodesk Combustion, Autodesk Discreet Flame

CREDITS
Director: Peter Thwaites
3D Director: Darren Walsh
Producers: Ben Link, Sally Heath
Lead Flame: Phil Oldham
Flame: Pete Smith
Combustion: Jonas Mouritsen

ADDIKT
THE NETHERLANDS
TITLE: KILL THE BILL
CLIENT: XS4ALL
FORMAT: WEB COMMERCIAL

PROFILE

Addikt was founded in 2004 in Amsterdam by Sander Lipmann, Koen van Ovoorde, and Barry Schwarz, whose backgrounds include graphic design, 3D design, and broadcast design.

Addikt focuses on motion-graphics design and 3D animation, with emphasis on the brand-design side of motion graphics. Instead of just selling a product, Addikt gives new impetus to a brand, or enhances something that's already present. It keeps in mind the core values of a brand, as well as highlighting aspects that are relevant to the target audience: "We create the style that fits the project ..."

STEPS TO CREATION

XS4ALL (Access for All) wanted to show off its VoIP (telephone via the Internet) service. With VoIP, there are no bills for phone calls. The idea was to depict a deathmatch-like movie, compared by two commentators, in which XS4ALL's Kill the Bill character beats up opponent Small Bill.

How would Small Bill be defeated? What kind of techniques would Kill the Bill use? The weapons used had to have something to do with modern phones but also needed to have an old-school look, and this was all worked out in the script. The writers came up with so much detail, and so many horrible scenarios for the two fighters, that the original allocation of one minute was expanded to just under thirty minutes.

As the script and storyboards were being edited, the illustrators worked on the skin and textures of the characters. They had to look as if they were made of clay, even though they were created in 3D. Once the script was finished, voices and images were laid on a timeline. All the rendering was completed in separate passes actually in front of the clients in order to make sure that it was done just as they wanted it.

TOOLS
Adobe After Effects, GenArts Sapphire Plug-ins, SoftimageXSI

CREDITS
Director: Koen van Ovoorde
Producers: Marleen Reen, Doet Bierma
Creative Team: Taco Zuiderma, Thomas Rouw
Character Design: Barry Schwarz, Koen van Ovoorde, Ilse Zaros
3D Modeling/Animation: Koen van Ovoorde, Adriano Zanetti, Katie Wilson, Sander Lipmann
Music/Sound Design: Larry Soundware

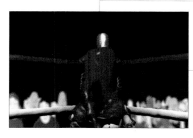

ADOLESCENT
USA
TITLE: COUNTRY FRIED HOME VIDEOS
CLIENT: CMT
FORMAT: TITLE SEQUENCE

PROFILE

Adolescent is a New York-based design studio with a strong international presence. The company's talented, multidisciplinary team brings innovative visions to its clients. Man-Wai Cheung, the creative director, states: "We are adolescent because we explore, experiment, and remain open to dynamic possibilities of expression."

Adolescent's work reflects the youthful, changing culture in urban environments and has a strong connection with emerging music scenes. Clients include Adidas, SVT1 in Sweden, VH1 US and UK, Space Shower TV in Japan, *Creative Review* magazine, and Cartoon Network.

Adolescent has also worked with MTV and Nickelodeon on the "Nag the Vote" campaign, designed to persuade children to urge their parents to vote; the "Let's Just Play" campaign, which encouraged kids to engage in activities other than watching television; and campaigns for the infamous SpongeBob SquarePants.

Television production company Levinson/Fontana chose Adolescent to create the title sequence for its series *The Bedford Diaries*. Adolescent's short film *DE05* was selected for the international film festival Resfest.

STEPS TO CREATION

Adolescent's collage-animation title sequence plays with iconic images of the United States, and features cutout characters caught in an absurd series of absurd accidents. The animation expresses the tone of the show: the self-effacing humor of the truly confident.

TOOLS
Adobe After Effects, Adobe Illustrator, Adobe Photoshop

CREDITS
Direction: Adolescent
Creative Director: Man-Wai Cheung
Art Director: Mina Muto
Design/Animation: Chris Stearns

ADOLESCENT
TITLE: IF YOUR NAME'S
        NOT DOWN
CLIENT: MTV DANCE UK
FORMAT: TITLE SEQUENCE

STEPS TO CREATION

If Your Name's Not Down, an interactive program on MTV Dance UK, features back-to-back videos of club hits, during which viewers' live text-to-screen messages scroll across the bottom of the screen.

Adolescent worked on three rounds of concepts before this one was approved. The sequence begins with a view of the planet Earth from space. A rhythmic beat slowly builds up as the camera zooms in on a brightly lit network of nightclubs. Technicolor parachutes and other free-floating objects pop into view and descend on the web of glittering nightclubs like a crowd gathering at the velvet ropes. Force fields appear that repel some of the objects, bouncing them back into space, while objects marked with a smiley-face logo are allowed in.

Storyboards were sketched, then the ideas were explored in 3D Studio Max to work out previsuals and create the most fun and dramatic camera moves to express the idea. Once the camera moves and basic elements had been established, the team experimented with different 3D elements. Compositing was done in After Effects, and many happy accidents occurred that were kept in the final sequence.

TOOLS
Adobe After Effects, Adobe Illustrator, Adobe Photoshop, Autodesk 3D Studio Max

CREDITS
Direction: Adolescent
Creative Director: Man-Wai Cheung
Art Director: Mina Muto
Animation: Gary Tam

ADOLESCENT
TITLE: NIGHT BLOCKS
CLIENT: TMF UK
FORMAT: NETWORK IDs

STEPS TO CREATION

When TMF, part of the MTV family in the UK, rebranded, it asked Adolescent to create a new family of IDs to introduce its evening and night programming. Adolescent's quirky animations were intended to help the transition from workaday life to the relaxing, cool, and music-filled evening that TMF had in store.

In each vignette, a scene from daily life (a parking garage, a shop window, a shower stall, a table cluttered with takeout containers, a view of the English countryside) is enlivened by colorful, abstract creatures that pop, zigzag, and bloom out of the dark corners to remind viewers to make time for music and imagination. The mix of realism and abstraction is futuristic and fun, and is well suited to the TMF audience, who are characterized as cheeky but down-to-earth and "in the know."

Some of the backgrounds were created as set designs; the parking garage was shot on location; and the countryside was a collage of different elements. The graphics were then animated over the back plates.

TOOLS
Adobe After Effects, Adobe Illustrator, Adobe Photoshop

CREDITS
Direction: Adolescent
Creative Director: Man-Wai Cheung
Art Director: Mina Muto
Animation: Gary Tam, Chris Stearns

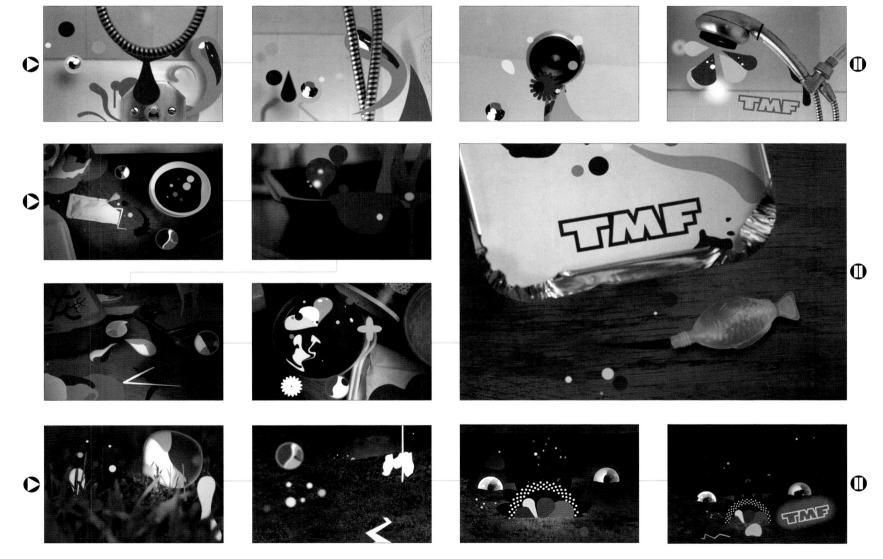

FILIPE ALÇADA
PORTUGAL
TITLE: AMPHIBIAN
CLIENT: PERSONAL PROJECT
FORMAT: SHORT FILM

PROFILE

Filipe Alçada is Portuguese, but he is based in London. He studied illustration at Kingston University, Surrey, England, where he made two animated shorts, after which he completed a masters degree in animation at the Royal College of Art in London.

After graduation, Alçada launched animation company Belzebu Films with Susi Wilkinson and Tess Laurence. Belzebu's first job was an animated music video for the band Add N to (X), and it won Best Music Video at the

New York Underground Film Festival. Other commissions for music videos soon followed, including work for the singer Moby, for which Belzebu not only won a double-platinum disc for contribution to sales of the album *Play*, but also a Best Music Video award at the World Animation Celebration festival in Los Angeles. Alçada, Wilkinson, and Laurence then joined production company Bermuda Shorts. Since then, Alçada's work as a director has included almost three hundred IDs for a rebrand of Nicktoons, a Nickelodeon digital channel.

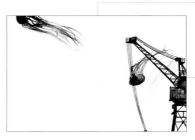

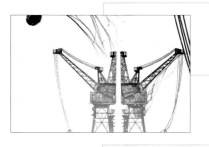
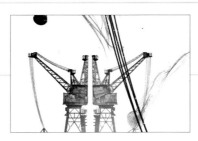

STEPS TO CREATION

While traveling around the world, Alçada compiled almost nine hours of live-action footage. *Amphibian* is a short film that grew out of an experiment incorporating this live action into Alçada's animation work.

The production process in this playful film was experimental, and the work was intended to be a vehicle for learning new techniques. The goal was to explore the potential of the footage and let the film develop naturally.

The first step was to select the best footage and treat it in such a way that the images became more abstract, which was achieved in Final Cut Express. Alçada took images of industrial sites on which he had worked in Photoshop and, using After Effects, added underwater footage. At first, the different types of files clashed. To blend the different elements, Alçada animated fog and snow to create a believable atmosphere and space.

Since Alçada was able to work on *Amphibian* only in his spare time and also learned to use the tools as he worked on the film, it took him three months to finish the project.

TOOLS
Adobe After Effects, Apple Final Cut Express, Macromedia Flash

CREDITS
Director: Filipe Alçada

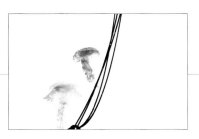

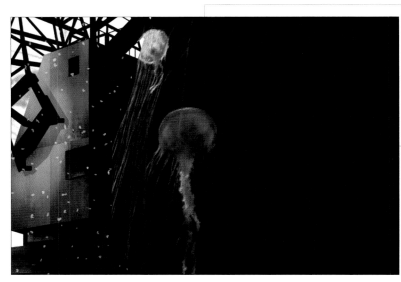
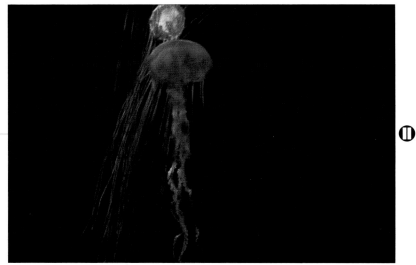

ARTHUR COX/TH1NG
UK
TITLE: KELLOGG'S ALL-BRAN BOOKSHELF
CLIENT: KELLOGG'S
FORMAT: TV COMMERCIAL

PROFILE

The Bristol-based company Arthur Cox was created in 2002, after founders Sarah Cox and Sally Arthur had worked together on Cox's award-winning short for Channel 4, *Plain Pleasures*. The company's distinctive style has been seen in ads for such clients as Dasani, Nestea, Coca-Cola, and Kellogg's.

Cox and Arthur respectively have also directed the award-winning short films *Heavy Pockets* and *Perfect*.

STEPS TO CREATION

This spot for Kellogg's, produced in collaboration with th1ng, illustrates how the concepts of fitness and healthy eating have changed in the twenty-five years since the publication of *The F-Plan Diet* by Audrey Eyton.

Each scene features bookshelves filled with bestsellers, health books, and visual scenarios of healthy eating and fitness. The scenarios are animated on the spines of the books and draw the viewer's eye naturally across the frame.

The technique of rotoscoping live action suits the ad, since it allows for clean lines and simple shapes.

Scenarios involving aerobics, yoga, and Frisbee-throwing were designed to fit into a long-panning shot, in which a woman's hand moves along the shelves.

Storyboards and designs were set to the rough soundtrack, and the directors worked to create the right rhythm for the concept. The team filmed a blue-screen shoot of all the actors, emphasizing clear outlines and strong shapes. The directors also took a series of hand shots in close-up; these were then transferred in 2K telecine to the postproduction department to be seamlessly joined. This formed the basis of a huge digital design, with graphically treated live action interacting with animated spines and text. The box of Kellogg's All-Bran Bran Flakes was positioned among the books and was pulled from the shelves in the same way as the other bestsellers, thereby emphasizing its place in a healthy lifestyle.

TOOLS
2K telecine, 16-mm film, Adobe After Effects, Adobe Photoshop, Apple Commotion Pro

CREDITS
Directors: Sarah Cox, Sally Arthur
Director of Photography: Sarah Bartles-Smith
Producer: Fiona Campbell/th1ng
CGI: Matthew Walker

AUGENBLICK STUDIOS
USA
TITLE: GOLDEN AGE/LANCASTER LOON
CLIENT: COMEDY CENTRAL
FORMAT: WEB CARTOON

PROFILE

Aaron Augenblick founded Augenblick Studios in Brooklyn, New York, in 1999. The company has produced a variety of works for television, film, and the Internet. Clients include MTV, Cartoon Network, Comedy Central, PBS, Nickelodeon, AT&T, and the director Spike Lee.

In addition to commercial projects, Augenblick Studios has created a string of critically acclaimed independent short films—*Ramblin' Man* (2000), *Drunky* (2001), and *Plugs McGinniss* (2003)—which have been shown at such international film festivals as Annecy, South by Southwest, and Slamdance. Its films have garnered numerous awards, including the Golden Gate Film Award, the ASIFA Award, the SXSW Animation Award, the DirecTV Award, and the Black Maria Juror's Citation Award.

Most recently, Augenblick Studios has created the animated content for two seasons of the absurdist *Wonder Showzen* comedy/variety show for MTV, which features puppets, kids, and cartoons. Augenblick Studios gained widespread notice for its spot-on

parodies of classic cartoons, and, in 2005, was named as one of the rising stars in the field by *Animation Magazine*.

STEPS TO CREATION

Augenblick Studios created the award-winning animated faux-documentary series *Golden Age*. Made up of ten segments, it features animated characters from the past.

Lancaster Loon follows the story of a mascot who stars in a string of TV commercials for the breakfast cereal Loony Puffs. In the commercials, three elves tease Lancaster Loon with a bowl of the sugary confection, driving him to increasing hysteria. His behavior resembles genuine psychosis.

The segment is a parody of such characters as Sonny the Cuckoo Bird (cartoon mascot for Cocoa Puffs), Trix Rabbit (Trix cereal), and Lucky the Leprechaun (Lucky Charms). The main concept was to take cartoon madness, which is presented as humorous to the viewer, and show

it as horrifying mental breakdown. The cereal itself is treated as a dangerous narcotic, such as heroin or crack cocaine. Eventually, the character ends up in a psychiatric hospital, attending self-help programs for obsessive cereal mascots.

The different eras of Loony Puff commercials are shown in *Lancaster Loon*, beginning with black-and-white ads from the 1950s, and continuing up to the colorful 1980s, when Lancaster Loon has his final meltdown. The idea that this character has enjoyed a long and successful career is endorsed through showing the viewer the subtle changes in film stock, color palette, and character design.

Written by Aaron Augenblick and Tim Harrod, the script includes all the narration and dialogue. Voice actors recorded the dialogue and narration for the segment, and a rough audio track was edited together. Storyboards were then drawn directly into the computer using a Wacom tablet, and were timed to the rough track. Characters and backgrounds were drawn with Flash

MX on a Wacom tablet. Much thought went into giving the style and line quality an organic, nondigital look.

Many sources were used for the images, including stock photography, vintage photographs, and pictures taken at the studio. Photoshop was used to manipulate photographs, in order to create as Aaron Augenblick explained, "artifacts of the cartoon character's existence in the 'real world'." Flash was used to animate the segment.

In an attempt to keep the vintage look authentic, the animator avoided using too many effects, such as motion-tweening and shape-tweening. The editor used After Effects to add such finishing touches as color balancing, aging, and camera blur.

TOOLS
Adobe After Effects, Adobe Audition, Adobe Photoshop, Adobe Premiere, Digidesign Pro Tools, Macromedia Flash, Motu Digital Performer, Wacom tablet

CREDITS
Director: Aaron Augenblick
Script: Aaron Augenblick, Tim Harrod
Animation: Chris Burns
Backgrounds: Jeremy Jusay
Photo Graphics: M. Wartella
Music: Bradford Reed

AUGENBLICK STUDIOS
TITLE: GOLDEN AGE/
MARCHING GUMDROP
CLIENT: COMEDY CENTRAL
FORMAT: WEB CARTOON

STEPS TO CREATION

Marching Gumdrop is another of the segments in the *Golden Age* series created by Augenblick Studios for Comedy Central. The primary theme of the series is the exposure of the supposed "dark underbelly" of seemingly innocuous cartoon characters.

    Marching Gumdrop follows the scandalous career of Jerome, a gumdrop from the Lobby Gang, a fictional group created by Aaron Augenblick and Tim Harrod

as a parody of the "Let's go out to the Lobby" movie-theater cartoon ads of the 1950s. The goal was to create a cartoon that evoked the feel and tone of the original cartoons strongly enough for the characters to seem familiar to the viewer.

    In *Marching Gumdrop*, Augenblick and Harrod present an animated Hollywood hell in which the über-cute Jerome, a perfectly sweet-natured everyman gumdrop, descends into various states of wretchedness, including alcoholism, drug dependency, and homelessness. Jerome is shown

in a variety of mocked-up television and movie clips. His story spans the 1950s to the 1990s, taking him from his heyday in the postwar era through a string of embarrassing career choices in the ensuing decades.

TOOLS + CREDITS

Marching Gumdrop went through the same developmental steps and procedures as *Lancaster Loon* (see page 30), and used the same tools, techniques, and software. Credits are also the same.

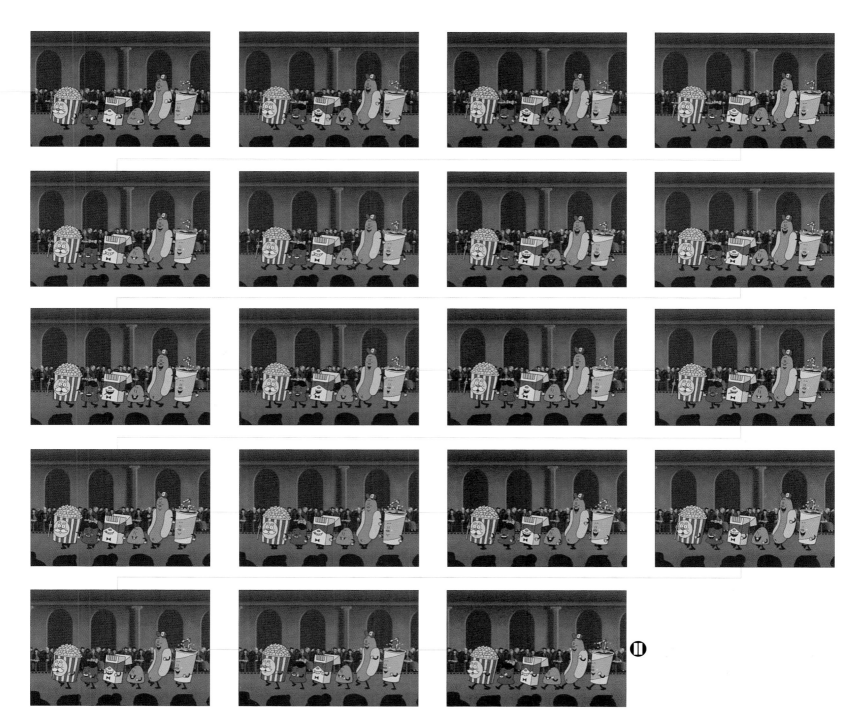

AUGENBLICK STUDIOS
TITLE: GOLDEN AGE/
        SKETCH TOWERS
CLIENT: COMEDY CENTRAL
FORMAT: WEB CARTOON

STEPS TO CREATION

Sketch Towers is different from the other segments in the Augenblick Studios' *Golden Age* series in that it does not focus on any single character, but instead homes in on a specific concept. The segment presents a range of animated characters, all physically or mentally damaged as a result of their very existence as drawn creatures. Half-drawn characters, or those that are flawed or mentally disturbed, are forced to live in a psychiatric hospital known as Sketch Towers.

Sketch Towers is clearly the darkest episode of the *Golden Age* series, and, as such, is treated in a more serious manner. The setting is a decaying hospital—a real-life former psychiatric hospital on Staten Island, New York, that is now an empty building—and it is presented as a genuinely dreadful place. The cartoon characters who live there are shimmering ghosts, locked away in this place for misfits.

The characters, which include a sketchy pencil test, a flip-book stick figure, and an experimental art project,

subsist in dank prison cells. One scene presents "the saddest cases of them all," disembodied cartoon pitches that never made it beyond the concept phase, which are seen as floating orbs of light in a shadowy padded room.

The final scene is meant not only to resolve this episode, but also to serve as an ending to the entire series. As the narrator rants about the forgotten cartoons that are ignored by the world at large, a dense parade of bizarre characters marches in unison. The narrator posits that these characters will someday "seek their revenge on the

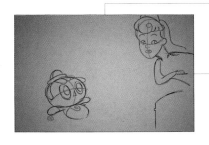

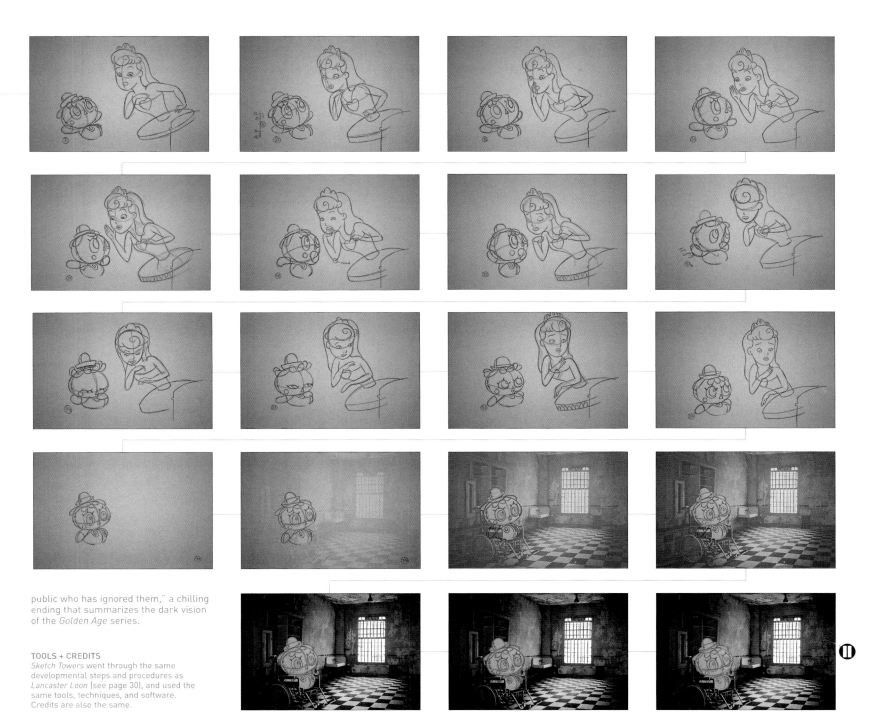

public who has ignored them," a chilling ending that summarizes the dark vision of the *Golden Age* series.

TOOLS + CREDITS
Sketch Towers went through the same developmental steps and procedures as *Lancaster Loon* (see page 30), and used the same tools, techniques, and software. Credits are also the same.

LIRON BAR-AKIVA
ISRAEL
TITLE: IT'S OH SO QUIET
CLIENT: PERSONAL PROJECT
FORMAT: SHORT FILM

PROFILE

Liron Bar-akiva is a graduate of the Bezalel Academy of Art and Design in Jerusalem. He has also studied film and TV production at Tel Aviv University.

STEPS TO CREATION

Bar-akiva said that the "Shhh ..." lyric from "It's Oh So Quiet" by Björk was the first idea that came into his mind when he was looking for a project for an animation course at the Bezalel Academy. He decided that he would use words as characters to illustrate the song. There followed months of brainstorming and years of production. The brief appearance of New York's World Trade Center in one shot dates the clip to before September 11, 2001.

Bar-akiva's objective was to balance the abstract typography and the figurative-narrative action. There is no story as such, but many dramatic situations convey the main theme in the song: "what's the use of falling in love?" The tough part was to keep bringing in new ideas without repeating anything.

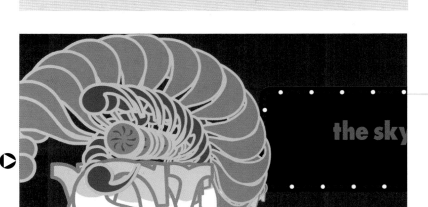

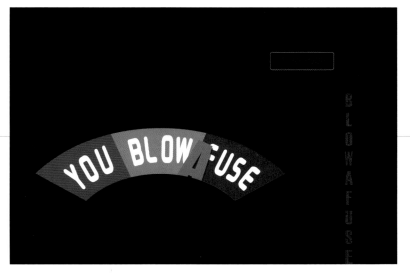

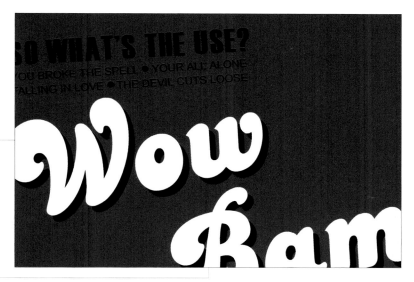

The film starts black and quiet, and then love comes in, bringing color and action. Typographical characters play the roles of quiet and noisy extremes, evoking the ups and downs of falling in love, while following the lyrics and the rhythmic fluctuation of the music.

Originally, Bar-akiva did the animation in Director, and then moved compositions around in Freehand. He captured the images—using screen capture—then moved them again and recaptured them, achieving a kind of computerized stop-motion. He subsequently discovered Flash and found it was the perfect tool for the project. Each shot was then animated in Flash and exported into Premiere for synchronizing and additional editing. A few minor adjustments were made in After Effects.

TOOLS
Adobe After Effects, Adobe Premiere, Macromedia Director, Macromedia Flash, Macromedia Freehand

CREDITS
Director/Producer: Liron Bar-akiva
Music: Björk

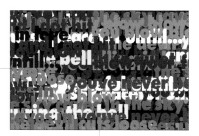

BL:ND
USA
TITLE: THE FINAL FU
CLIENT: MTV2
FORMAT: TITLE SEQUENCE

PROFILE

Established in 1995, Bl:nd (pronounced "blind") is a full-service design, production, and postproduction company with a folio that includes editorial work and live-action directing for commercials, broadcast TV, and film. Located in Santa Monica, at the heart of the postproduction community, Bl:nd employs a team of award-winning designers, animators, editors, and filmmakers. It has accrued numerous industry accolades and has assembled an enviable list of international clients.

STEPS TO CREATION

MTV2's Justin Rosenblatt asked Bl:nd to come up with an opening for his martial arts competition series, The Final Fu, that would both explain the premise of the show and be exciting to watch.

The main focus was to create through animation a believable fight scene that would electrify viewers with the visceral excitement of the sport as well as evoke nostalgia for the kung fu cinema and anime of the past.

The initial character designs and backgrounds were roughed out

But There Can Only Be One

in pen and pencil and rendered and painted in Photoshop. Each character was developed from every possible angle to help the 3D modeling team. The characters were modeled and rigged in Studio Max. The background scenes were 2D matte paintings, animated in 2D and imported onto 3D geometry.

TOOLS
Adobe After Effects, Adobe Illustrator, Adobe Photoshop, Autodesk 3D Studio Max, pen and ink

CREDITS
Director: Thomas Koh
Executive Producers: Santino Sladavic, Hilary Wright
Design/Illustration: Thomas Koh, Mike Lee, Lance Laspina
Animation: Lawrence Wyatt, Thomas Koh, Atsushi Ishizuka, Lance Laspina, Amit Doron
3D Modeling: Benji Schupp, Lawrence Wyatt

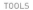

BL:ND
TITLE: HAPPY ENTRAILS
CLIENT: SPECIALIZED
FORMAT: WEB COMMERCIAL

STEPS TO CREATION

The bike company Specialized wanted a character animation to promote its newly designed mountain bike, the Stumpjumper, in its online ad campaign.

Bl:nd created a sixty-second story about a mountain biker who takes a wrong turn on a ride, which leads him down a path to utter destruction. Nothing seems to stop the biker or his bike, not even attacks by flesh-tearing grizzly bears and eye-gouging birds. Initially, viewers are lulled into thinking that they are watching an innocent and harmless animation. They are, therefore, extremely surprised and challenged when the story begins to unfold.

The first step in the creation of this concept was the extensive development of all of the characters featured in the spot. Each character was designed to appear cute and unthreatening, in order to set up the chain of events. The spot was created to resemble an old cartoon pulled from the archives of *Saturday Morning*, which made it easier to create a seemingly innocent, idyllic landscape and contrast it with the menacing behavior of the other characters toward the biker. It was important for the violence and gore to be raw and believable, in order for the viewer to feel the effect of what the biker was experiencing.

The characters were roughed out in pen and pencil, and tightened and colored in Illustrator and Photoshop. Most of the character animations were cel animation from the ground up. Other animations were roughed out in Studio Max, which created a visual guide on which to draw. Maya and Cinema 4D were used to create various additional elements, such as the fire at the end of the commercial.

TOOLS
Adobe After Effects, Adobe Illustrator,
Adobe Photoshop, Autodesk 3D Studio Max,
Autodesk Maya, Maxon Cinema 4D, pen
and pencil

CREDITS
Director: Thomas Koh
Producers: Santino Sladavic, Amy Knerl
Design/Illustration: Thomas Koh, Bill Sneed,
Joseph Chan

BUCK
USA
TITLE: FAMILY
CLIENT: CINGULAR WIRELESS
FORMAT: TV COMMERCIAL

PROFILE

Ryan Honey and Jeff Ellermeyer came together in the spring of 2003 to form Buck, a motion-graphics, design, and production studio based in Los Angeles. The company name was inspired by the designer Buckminster Fuller, best known for developing the geodesic dome in the late 1940s, but also a great innovator in the fields of art and science.

Honey assembled a creative team of designers, animators, editors, and directors from around the world. The company continued to grow, and in 2006

added a New York office and a third partner, Orion Tait.

Buck's directors and artists employ animation, visual effects, and live action, and work in collaboration with clients from concept to delivery, to produce innovative and diverse work.

STEPS TO CREATION

This spot was the second in a series of three ads for Cingular Wireless (now AT&T). The first ad, which had been produced a year earlier, helped shape

the campaign. Artists, keen to get started on *Family*, sorted through a mountain of ideas and illustrations. Eventually, they put together a script that fulfilled both Buck's creative desires and the client's needs— something that's not always easy to achieve.

The look was to be that of a modernist cartoon world, using oversized shapes with a hard modern edge. In most cases, Photoshop artists treated and altered each set of renders before they were composited. In that way the team were not tied down to the renders and were able to maintain full control over the look.

The job schedule was cut by more than half soon after production began and it took quick thinking, clever storytelling, and exceptional creative resources to meet every expectation.

Written treatments, boards, and an animatic were prepared. Following feedback from the client, a more detailed animatic and a series of drawn studies were completed for the main characters. At this point, modelers began work, followed a few days later by animators, who began with stand-in rigs. Processes such as shading were carried out simultaneously in the background. The easiest shots were completed first, and the company established a strict schedule for finalizing them. This gave Buck enough time to work out any inconsistencies.

Next, the shots were finalized so that animation could be baked out. Select still-frame passes were rendered and a specific look was created for them in Photoshop. Once approved, any 2D tricks were translated back into 3D shaders so that passes could be rendered. From there, cameras were brought into the composing software, along with numerous passes.

TOOLS
Adobe After Effects, Adobe Photoshop, Apple Final Cut Pro, Autodesk Maya, proprietary techniques

CREDITS
Directors: Ryan Honey, Jeremy Sahlman
Art Director: Thomas Schmid
Producers: Maurie Enochson, Nick Terzich
Design: Yker Moreno, Ben Langsfeld, Stephen Kelleher
3D Animation: Steve Day, John Nguyen, Shannon Pytlak, Jim Richardson, Karen Soh, Henry Foster
3D Modeling: Jens Lindgren, Karen Soh, Henry Foster, Paul America, Joel Anderson, Brandon Perlow
Texturing/Lighting: Bill Dorais
Compositing: Patrick Scruggs, Brad Gayo
Editor: Harry Walsh

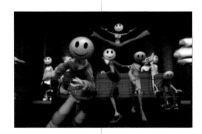

BUCK
TITLE: X-PLAY
CLIENT: G4 MEDIA
FORMAT: TITLE SEQUENCE

STEPS TO CREATION

The G4 network wanted to produce a cel-animated show package for its video-game review program, X-Play, hosted by Adam Sessler and Morgan Webb. G4 wanted Buck to follow up the program's hand-drawn style, and see how well it could integrate the two hosts into an illustrated video-game scenario. At the time, many 3D cartoons were being produced, but Buck was more interested in the loosely drawn looks used by Katsuji Morishita (who had done the animated sequence in Kill Bill:

Volume 1) and Shinichirô Watanabe (The Animatrix series: Kid's Story). Those pieces branched out of the strict and exact anime genre. The characters didn't seem truly consistent frame to frame, and the animation techniques added a lot of style and life to the motion. Buck added a spin by introducing its own drawing style, and bought a hand-painted feel to the highlights and textures in the background.

To distinguish this piece from Buck's other cel animation, these animations were done in rough pencil style, with no inking. This allowed the illustration some

freedom from proportional exactness, and it sped up tremendously the production of drawings. Similarly, since no time was spent inking, more effects and sequences were able to be incorporated into the project.

The unique look was heightened by hand-painting the highlights, frame by frame, with a brush technique that fractured continuity between frames. When characters distorted and bent in motion, it was easy to match the animation appeal with this looser paint style. Any color was treated with layered washes, so that the highlights and

scratchiness of the characters were consistent with the world around them. Ultimately, the end result rode the line between graphic novel and anime.

The futuristic world in which Sessler and Webb shoot at each other presented a challenge. To make the "first-person shooter" genre believable, the camera had to be positioned in such a way that it would record from the viewpoint of a character, and the film had to feel like 3D. A CGI environment had to be used, but CGI renders don't always have as much character as hand-painted backgrounds, unless

there is time to hand-paint every texture within that world, as in *Metropolis* and *Steamboy*. The use of a couple of shaders and manipulation of lighting schemes helped push the traditional 3D-look into a style of its own, however. To tie it all together, an accelerated dubstep track was added, which brought a contemporary feel to the sound score. It proved to be so exciting that dialogue wasn't deemed necessary in the end.

TOOLS
Adobe Photoshop, Adobe After Effects

CREDITS
Director: Orion Tait
Art Director: Thomas Schmid
Producers: Maurie Enochson, Cassandra Khavari, Nick Terzich
Design: Steve Pacheco, Ben Langsfeld
Animation: Morgan James, Patrick Scruggs
Editor: Harry Walsh
Music/Sound Design: Cypher Audio

CA-SQUARE
USA
TITLE: VSPOT BRAND PACKAGE
CLIENT: VH1
FORMAT: TV COMMERCIAL

PROFILE

CA-Square provides strategic and creative image-enhancing solutions for some of the world's most successful media and entertainment companies. In partnership with its clients, CA-Square plans, designs, and implements cross-platform, multicountry, multilingual communications that shape the way people perceive a brand and interact with it.

Over the past few years, CA-Square has created broadcast identity packages for such global brands as Disney and Fox. Other clients include VH1, Reuters, Telemundo, AT&T, AMG, Mercedes-Benz, Garnier Fructis, Queer Dharma, and Lego.

STEPS TO CREATION

VSpot is a broadband entertainment network that provides an interactive user experience. The challenge here was how to communicate the web experience to a TV audience. Animation was used to tell the story, and a futuristic interface was developed to

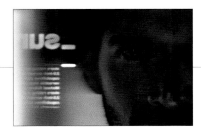

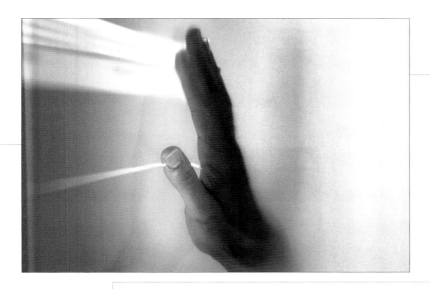

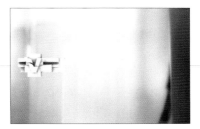

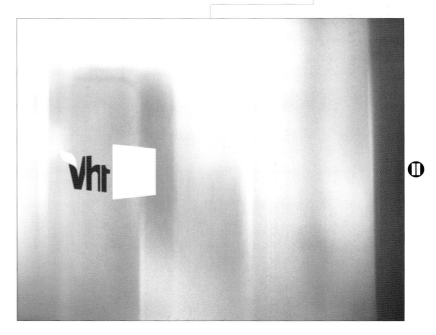

suggest a high level of customization and the use of all three dimensions in equal measure. As a user chose a navigational element, translucent panels slid out to reveal underlying options.

Many projects follow a linear production path, but time constraints demanded parallel development on this commercial. While one team used SoftimageXSI to animate the logo, which deconstructs in three-dimensional space, another group of artists and designers developed textures, structures, and shapes that would form the basis of the architecture and navigation system. Meanwhile, a third group was exploring duotones, developing an overall color palette, and creating layouts for the numerous sequences.

While the logo animation was underway, a series of mood boards were created for the client to review. Once the look and feel of the package had been established, the team created animatics to determine how the pieces would flow.

CA-Square developed a set of detailed shooting boards. During this process, the production team created graphic panels that were output to sheets of Plexiglas. These panels were used as props during the shoot, and eventually helped tie together the live-action imagery with the 3D-CGI elements. The action was shot in high definition to allow greater flexibility during the postproduction process. HD technology also allowed greater latitude with regard to color correction, framing, and the creation of invisible composites.

TOOLS
Adobe Illustrator, Adobe Photoshop, Apple Final Cut Pro, Maxon Cinema 4D, NewTek LightWave 3D, SoftimageXSI

CREDITS
Director: Amanda Havey
Creative Director: Robert A. Grobengieser
Director of Photography: Robert Aumer
Producer: Dave Perry
Animation/Compositing: David DiMeola
3D CGI: Walter Lubinski, Jason Strougo

JENNIFER A. CABLE
USA
TITLE: TIME AND SEQUENCE PROJECT
CLIENT: PERSONAL PROJECT
FORMAT: SHORT FILM

PROFILE

Jennifer A. Cable received her BSc
degree in graphic design from the
Pennsylvania State University in 2006.
Her work was selected for The Real
Show sponsored by the Art Directors
Club of Metropolitan Washington, in
2005, the Graphis New Talent Design
Annual 2006, and the 2006 Annual
National Student Show, sponsored
by the Dallas Society of Visual
Communications.

STEPS TO CREATION

Cable's course assignment was to select
a soundtrack and create appropriate
imagery for it by manipulating 16-mm
film. She found it fairly easy to create
hard, edgy graphics by scratching and
coloring the surface of the film. Cable
looked for soft, melodic piano music to
challenge herself. She chose Aphex
Twin's "Avril 14th," which has a simple
melody that evolves and then repeats
itself at the end.
    It was Easter when Cable was
working on this project, and her family

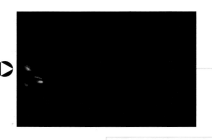   

 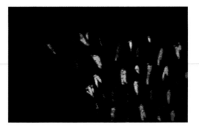 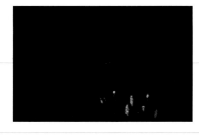 

 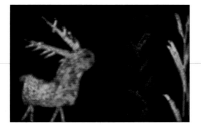  

  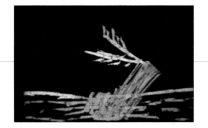 

was making Pysanky eggs (traditional Ukrainian decorated Easter eggs). Many Pysanky eggs are decorated with such simple images as wheat, trees, birds, and deer, which are often combined to tell stories relating to the cycle of nature. Cable felt this related well to the music.

After studying the soundtrack, Cable began sketching storyboards to figure out the best sequence of images. She began with a few birds that multiply to become a large, colorful flock. When the birds fly to the bottom of the screen, three shafts of wheat grow in their place. A deer comes along and eats the wheat, taking on the color of the crop. It runs off in time to the music and merges into the ground, where a tree blooms and bursts into different colors. The colors turn into the flock of birds originally seen at the beginning of the piece. The birds then merge to form a drop of water that falls and splashes off the screen.

Cable practiced by scratching images on scrap pieces of film, which she ran through a projector to see how they looked. She continued working until she had a set of images that she could use as guides in making the final version. Next, Cable imported the soundtrack file into Sound Studio. Since a projector shows 16-mm film at twenty-four frames per second, she set up guides at this ratio, which allowed her to hear all the sounds present in each corresponding frame of the film. She counted out the frames into groups of twenty-four, marking out every second.

Using an X-Acto knife, Cable scratched away at the film's black emulsion to mark the main events, after which she added detail and color. The tree posed the biggest challenge. Cable scanned an ink drawing of the tree into a computer, printed it on to hundreds of clear office labels, then stuck these to clear 16-mm film. Finally, Cable scratched away the stickers and added the bursts of color.

TOOLS
16-mm film, clear office labels, Freeverse Sound Studio, permanent markers, X-Acto knife

CREDITS
All work: Jennifer A. Cable
This project was an assignment in Professor Sommese's senior graphic design class, "Time and Sequence."

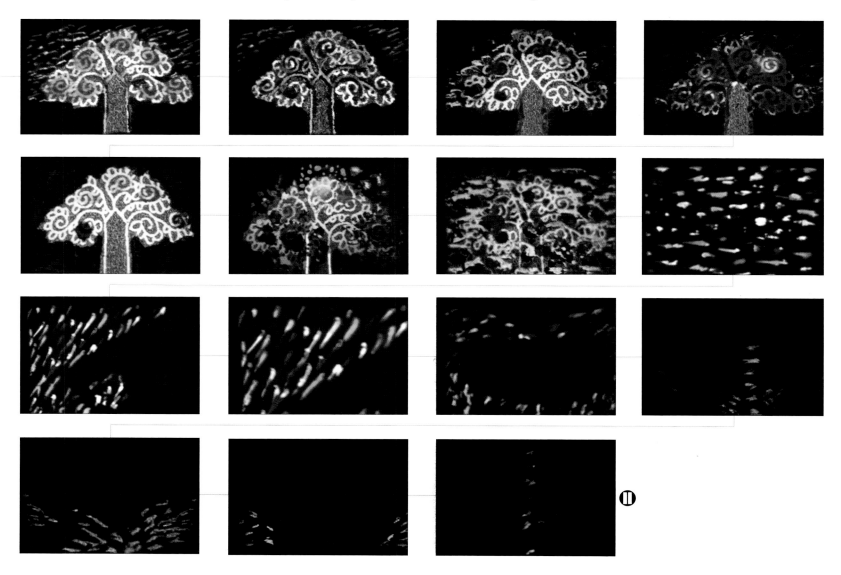

CHAOTIC UNICORN
USA
TITLE: DANCER
CLIENT: NICKTOONS
FORMAT: TV COMMERCIAL

PROFILE

Euralis Weekes and Tasayu Tasnaphun, the founders of Chaotic Unicorn (CU), are graduates of New York's School of Visual Arts. CU's energy is drawn mainly from Weekes's experience in the entertainment industry and Tasnaphun's edgy, eastern vibe, gained during time spent in Japan and Thailand. CU operates in New York City and Japan. Clients include Viacom, JVC, and Thai hip-hop group SEA.

STEPS TO CREATION

This spot was intended to make viewers check out the "Dancer" Flash game on the Nicktoons website. Euralis Weekes's main challenge was incorporating and blending the work of Alexandre Houden, the game's designer and animator, into the spot in an engaging and memorable way. Thematically, the MGM movie musicals of the late 1940s to mid-1950s seemed to fit, and CU created a quick storyboard on Post-it notes, mapping out every conceivable funny visual.

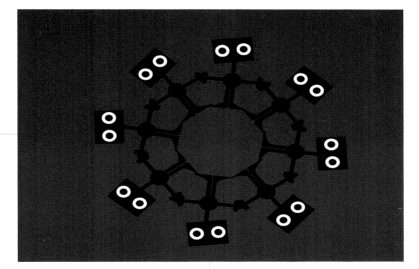

Scenes, including those featuring circles of people performing synchronized swimming in a pool and characters snapping their fingers to the beat, were referenced from old musicals. The scenes were drawn out, shot-for-shot, on Post-it notes, which were stuck on a wall. The notes were then shuffled around until the best sequence of events was found. A fast and upbeat techno track was selected to make the spot more attractive.

Snapz Pro, a video-capture program, captured the dances that the characters performed. These loopable little dances were then laid into shots according to the boards. The clips were timed to the music, and all the final composites were rendered in After Effects.

TOOLS
Adobe After Effects, Adobe Illustrator, Adobe Photoshop, Ambrosia Snapz Pro, Apple Final Cut Pro, Apple Shake, Corel Painter, Macromedia Flash, pencil and paper

CREDITS
Producer/Animation: Euralis Weekes
Dancer Design: Alexandre Houden
Music Supplier: Extreme Music

CHAOTIC UNICORN
TITLE: JVC FESTIVAL OPENING
CLIENT: JVC JAZZ FESTIVAL
FORMAT: TV COMMERCIAL

STEPS TO CREATION

One of Chaotic Unicorn's biggest challenges was to produce a fifteen-second ad for the 2005 JVC Jazz Festival that would also show off JVC's electronics lineup for 2006. The turnaround time was less than two weeks.

After a day of brainstorming and storyboarding, CU developed a set of highly stylistic Euro-pop images. A series of lines carried the concept across the spot as a whole, and special colors highlighted the products.

Key composites were filmed with a digital camcorder, and the footage was imported into Final Cut Pro. A rough cut was built to sort out the timing and to check the flow, and final timings and tweaks were implemented. Once the shots were laid out, the background was built using Adobe Illustrator. Concurrently, another animator was rotoscoping the live footage in Shake. In an effort to save time, the car was rendered in Maya, using a 'toon shader to fit the final design. The various elements were composited in After Effects, which took a day to render.

TOOLS
Adobe After Effects, Adobe Illustrator, Adobe Photoshop, Apple Final Cut Pro, Apple Shake, Autodesk Maya, Corel Painter, Macromedia Flash, pencil and paper

CREDITS
Directors: Tasayu Tasnaphun, Euralis Weekes
Production: Festival Productions
3D Animation: Jeremy Fernsler

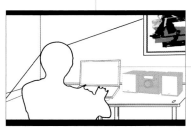

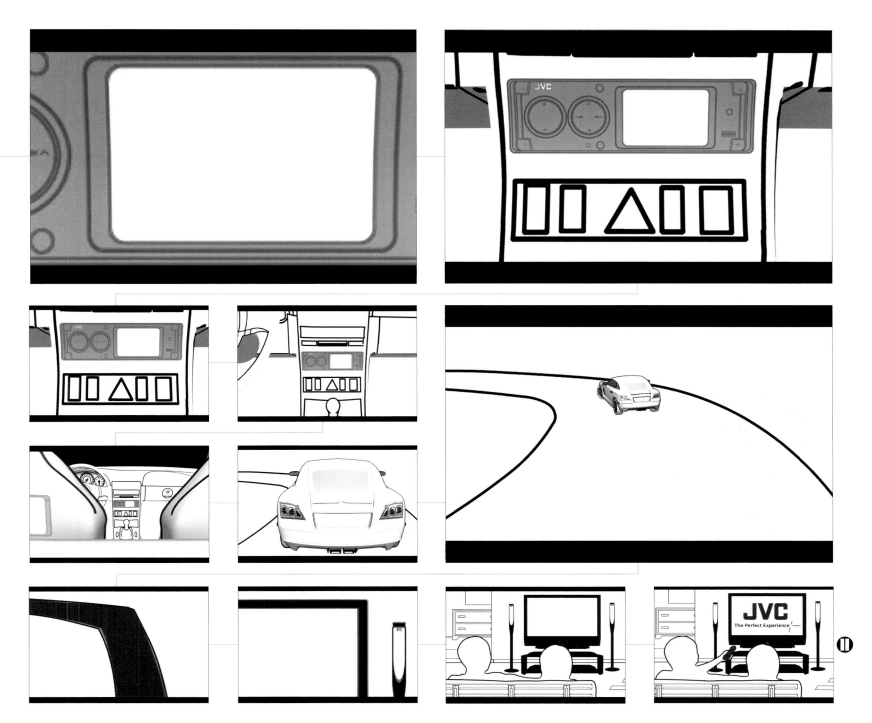

CHAOTIC UNICORN
TITLE: SNOWMAN MELTDOWN
CLIENT: NICKTOONS
FORMAT: NETWORK IDs

STEPS TO CREATION

Commissioned to do twelve spots for Nicktoons's winter-programming package, Chaotic Unicorn split the assignment between its two founders. Euralis Weekes opted for traditional animation, while Tasayu Tasnaphun explored computer-mimicked paper-cutout animation.

The traditional animation spots were constructed by scanning every hand-drawn and inked frame into Photoshop for some artistic color toning. The final renders were done in After Effects.

The construction-paper-style spots were achieved by scanning in various paper textures and hand-drawn animation. These were painstakingly composited and constructed in Photoshop, then animated in After Effects. The use of a Wacom tablet helped speed up the creative process.

TOOLS
Adobe After Effects, Adobe Illustrator, Adobe Photoshop, Apple Final Cut Pro, Apple Shake, Corel Painter, Macromedia Flash, pencil and paper, Wacom tablet

CREDITS
Production: Nicktoons
Animation: Euralis Weekes, Tasayu Tasnaphun, Erik Chichester

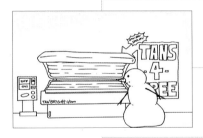

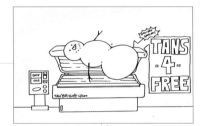

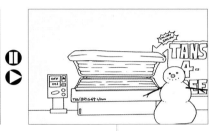
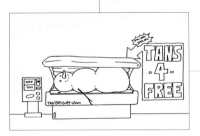

SYLVAIN CHOMET/TH1NG
UK
TITLE: TOMORROW
CLIENT: WINTERTHUR
FORMAT: TV + FILM COMMERCIAL

PROFILE

Sylvain Chomet was born in France in 1963, and graduated from the art school of Angoulême in 1987. He now lives in Scotland, where his studio, Django Films, is based. In 1997, Chomet's first animated short, *La Vieille Dame et les pigeons* (Old Lady and Pigeons) was nominated for an Academy Award. In 2004, his first feature film, *Les Triplettes de Belleville* (more popularly known as *Belleville-Rendezvous*) was again nominated by the Academy, this time for two awards. *Tomorrow*, the project featured here, was coordinated by th1ng production company.

STEPS TO CREATION

According to Chomet, every good commercial begins with an original script that allows room for collaboration with its director. *Tomorrow* was no exception. The people of a town called Today are frightened by a monster called Tomorrow, until they are reassured by the Winterthur insurance company and come to befriend Tomorrow.

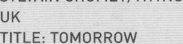

Chomet and his team began by roughing out a storyboard and developing designs. The storyboard stage of an animated piece is a very creative part of the process, in which visual ideas become reality: the creeping shadow building the tension, the fireworks, and the style of movement were all developed during storyboarding. Chomet visualized the Tomorrow monster as moving strangely, in a way that set him apart from the rest of the characters. The monster moved smoothly and slowly, helping create a sense of mystery and eeriness.

The layouts and characters were developed from the storyboards, and original sketches were drawn on paper. The animation was divided: all the human characters were animated by hand, on paper; the monster was animated using inbetweening computer software, which helped lend his movement an otherworldly feel. The car and the fireworks at the end of the commercial were also animated in CGI.

The hand-drawn work was colored digitally, while the CGI car was colored using 'toon shading to make it feel like drawn animation. The monster was constructed as a transparent matte through which the background was visible. The line work for the backgrounds was drawn by hand and colored in Photoshop to imitate watercolor. All these elements were composited to form the near-final image. Finally, the film was color corrected and the titles added.

The animation for *Tomorrow* took twelve weeks to complete, the coloring took three, and the compositing two.

TOOLS
Adobe After Effects, Adobe Photoshop, Autodesk Maya, Cambridge Animation System Animo, pencil and paper

CREDITS
Director/Animation: Sylvain Chomet
Creative Director: Keith Loell
Producers: Sedonie Adams-Grant, Dominic Buttimore

RASTKO ĆIRIĆ
SERBIA
TITLE: METAMORPH
CLIENT: MINISTRY OF CULTURE, BELGRADE
FORMAT: SHORT FILM

PROFILE

Rastko Ćirić was born in Belgrade, Serbia. He is a professor of illustration and animation at the University of Arts in Belgrade, and founded the animation studio at its faculty of applied arts; he is also head of the Digital Art Group of its interdisciplinary PhD studies program.

Ćirić has illustrated for the *New York Times Book Review* since 2002. He has written and designed many illustrated books, mounted thirty solo exhibitions, and created thirteen animated films.

STEPS TO CREATION

Metamorph presents itself as a documentary film, but since it is about an imaginary creature, Ćirić decided to use animation. The film is an instruction guide for cultivating a creature that during its life cycle, changes so radically that it exhibits characteristics of almost every living being.

The project started as an illustrated booklet called *Home-Bred Metamorph Cultivating Manual*. Steven Heller, Ćirić's editor at the *New York Times*, saw the booklet and suggested that

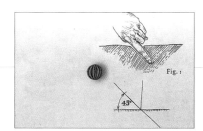

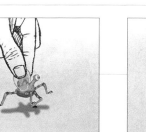
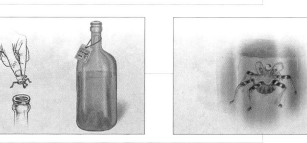

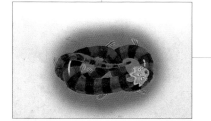

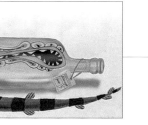

he make it into an animated film. Thus, *Metamorph* came to form part of both a film trilogy and a multimedia project that included an illustrated book and a solo exhibition.

Financed by the Serbian Ministry of Culture, the film was created through a combination of drawing with soft pencil on paper and Ćirić's technique of painting with oil on glass and celluloid. It took a year to execute. Everything was photographed with a digital camera and the images were imported into a Mac. All the pictures were processed in Photoshop and edited in Final Cut.

It was a computer-finished process, but Ćirić hoped to achieve the look of the painted bestiaries of the eighteenth century. All the sounds were created by Svetolik Mica Zajc.

Ćirić dedicated the film to a good friend of his, the director Milenko Štrbac (1925–2004), a pioneer of Serbian documentary film, who had advised Ćirić since his first film but would never allow his name to be mentioned in the credits. During the two men's last meeting, Štrbac told Ćirić that he should finish this film without the "compromises and mistakes" he had

accepted on previous films but now regretted. Ćirić hopes he has fulfilled his friend's last wish.

TOOLS
Adobe Photoshop, Apple Final Cut Pro, pencil and paper

CREDITS
Director/Producer/Animator: Rastko Ćirić
Music/Soundtrack: Svetolik Mica Zajc

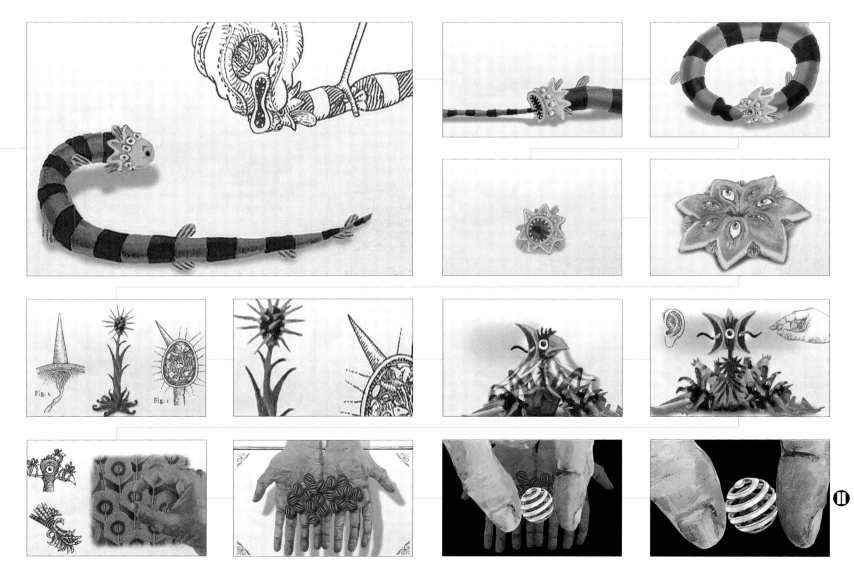

CLICK 3X
USA
TITLE: LIVING THINGS, "BOM BOM BOM"
CLIENT: JIVE RECORDS
FORMAT: MUSIC VIDEO

PROFILE

New York-based Click 3x fuses strategic and creative thinking to produce visual solutions for advertising agencies, broadcasters, and some of the world's best-known brands. The studio provides visual effects, computer animation, design, and editorial services. Since its foundation in 1994, Click 3x has gone on to become one of the industry's leading creative entities. Recent collaborations include work for Samsung, MTV/Virgin, Meijer, New Balance, Miller Brewing, Lugz, Zero 7, and Time Warner.

STEPS TO CREATION

This project was a collaborative effort between the video's director, Floria Sigismondi, and Click 3x. It was decided early on that the look of the video would be reminiscent of the vibrant artwork popular in the 1970s.

Experimentation on a series of still frames to test different approaches resulted in the development of a multi-stage technique to treat the live-action footage so that it combined detail with a hallucinatory sensibility. The look of the imagery was created in Photoshop.

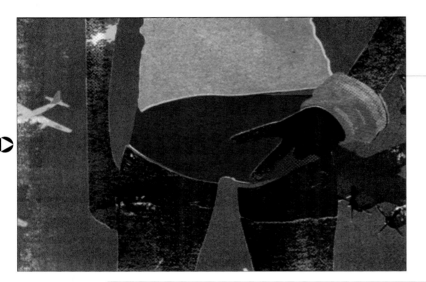

The second phase of production used Flame and After Effects to cut mattes, treat the footage, and create transitional effects and animated backdrops on which to build compositions. In the meantime, the CGI team had generated models in 3D Studio Max, which were then imported into Flame and texture-mapped. Numerous hours went into tweaking the look, giving each scene a unique painted quality.

TOOLS
Adobe After Effects, Adobe Illustrator, Adobe Photoshop, Autodesk 3D Studio Max, Autodesk Flame

CREDITS
Director: Floria Sigismondi (Revolver Film Company)
Animation: Click 3x
Additional Animation: Susan Armstrong
Contributing Artist: Steve Wilson
Music: Living Things

CLICK 3X
TITLE: SAMSUNG E720 "SPIN"
CLIENT: SAMSUNG
FORMAT: TV COMMERCIAL

STEPS TO CREATION

When the ad agency JWT needed a dynamic thirty-second spot to showcase a stylish new Samsung mobile phone with camera and MP3 player—both market-leading features at the time— it called Click 3x.

Click 3x presented a rather unorthodox solution, one that used stylish illustration to take viewers on a journey through the phone's remarkable features.

Having finalized the idea, the design team set about developing storyboards.

They decided on two distinct styles of music: classical and rock. Once the music was finished, the animators began synchronizing their images and the music. Fingers dance on piano keys in the classical sequence, and fly across guitar frets in the rock-'n'-roll section. The design team also created a distinct color palette for each section: cool blues and violets for classical music, and blistering reds and oranges for rock. These colors fill the shapes that serve as both background elements and transitional elements, segueing in and out of the sequence.

To complete the puzzle, a photo-real version of the phone was created and animated. The phone element was crucial, as it provided the perspective of entering and exiting the music via the built-in lens.

TOOLS
Adobe Illustrator, Adobe Photoshop, Autodesk 3D Studio Max, Autodesk Flame

CREDITS
Design/Animation: Click 3x
Music: Human

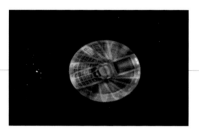
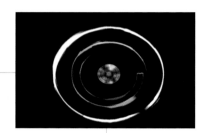

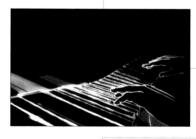
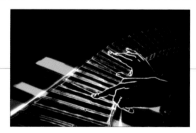
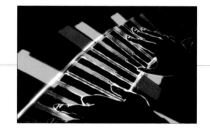

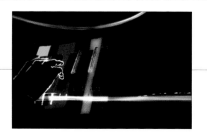

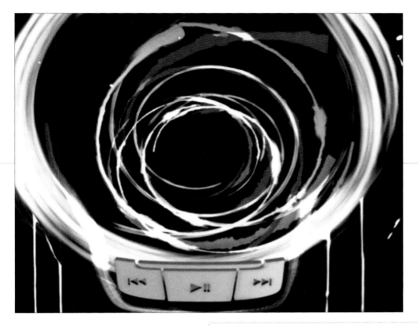
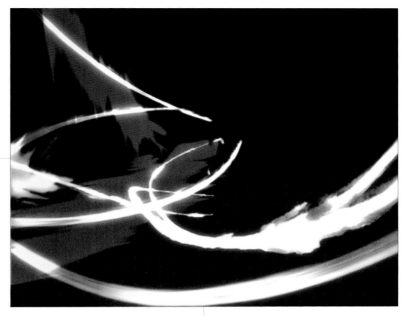
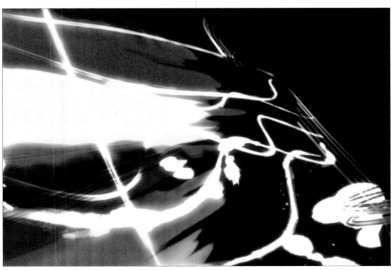

CURIOUS PICTURES
USA
TITLE: SELECCIÓN
CLIENT: TOYOTA MEXICO
FORMAT: TV COMMERCIAL

PROFILE

Curious Pictures was founded in 1993 by partners Susan Holden, Steve Oakes, David Starr, and Richard Winkler. It is the largest animation studio in New York City and the home of award-winning creators of animated series, commercials, and celebrated characters in picture books and on television. Curious Pictures produces such acclaimed hit TV shows as *Little Einsteins* for Disney, *Codename: Kids Next Door* and *Sheep in the Big City* for the Cartoon Network, *A Little Curious* for HBO, and *Avenue Amy* for the Oxygen network. Its directors have won two Academy Award nominations, eighteen Emmy Awards, and two Caldecott Honors, and have four commercials in the permanent collection of New York's Museum of Modern Art.

Using its multiple strengths in animation, design, production, and brand strategy, Curious also creates successful branded entertainment for Mattel and AOL, as well as commercials for such clients as Toyota, American Express, Coca-Cola, Pepsi, Target, Burger King, McDonald's, Dunkin' Donuts, Best Buy, the Sundance Channel, and hundreds more.

STEPS TO CREATION

The job was a branding and sponsorship exercise for Toyota Mexico and illustrated the evolution of transport through the ages.

The spot begins at the dawn of time and journeys through early mythological beliefs, the mapping of the Earth and stars, and Leonardo da Vinci's theoretical mechanical designs to the evolution of the motorcar and Toyota's vision of future energy-efficient cars.

The biggest problem was finding a visual style that illustrated the passage of centuries but maintained a cohesive look throughout the ad. Elements were drawn from such diverse sources as old celestial maps, blueprints, alchemical etchings, Victorian industrial designs, and the film work of Eadweard Muybridge and Georges Méliès. To avoid giving too much of a cold, modern

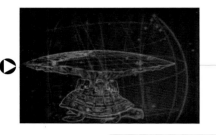

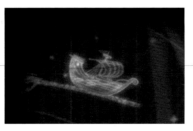

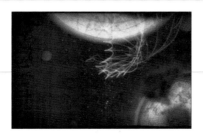

technological feel to the present-day segment, the look of old daguerreotype photographs was combined with dark, smudgy blueprints. This provided the thread that linked everything together. The overall feel and look started to evolve, producing a spot that seemed as if it had been recovered from some murky archive.

Each scene was designed in Photoshop. The various elements were layered using combinations of opacity and blending mode to get the dark, antique look. The images were then taken into After Effects, where many

of the various elements were animated. The live elements were shot by Cuatro Y Medio, using banks of still cameras and Flash in a method similar to the one Muybridge would have employed in the late nineteenth century, except that in some cases the actors were shot against blue screen. These images were assembled in Final Cut, imported into After Effects, and added into the Photoshop imagery.

The 3D components were made in 3D Studio Max, while the various pieces of 2D animation were animated by hand on paper in the traditional way and

included as an additional layer. For the final stage, the composited footage was taken into Flame so that a distressed film look could be applied.

TOOLS
Adobe After Effects, Adobe Illustrator, Adobe Photoshop, Apple Final Cut Express, Autodesk 3D Studio Max, Autodesk Discreet Flame, pencil and paper

CREDITS
Director: Flea Circus
Animation: John Robertson
Sound Design: Jacobo Liberman

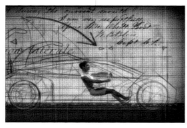
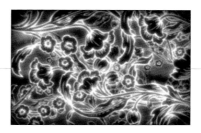

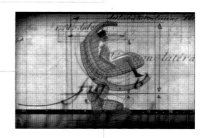
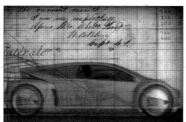

CURIOUS PICTURES
TITLE: TURTLE
CLIENT: VOLKSWAGEN
FORMAT: WEB COMMERCIAL

STEPS TO CREATION

Curious Pictures was contacted by the Arnold Agency to develop a concept for a website for the 2006 Volkswagen Passat. The car had 120 new features, and the agency wanted to create short metaphorical movies for each of them. It awarded Curious Pictures nine spots, including one that was meant to be a metaphor for precision laser-welded seams—not the easiest of tasks.

Curious Pictures works by throwing a pool of ideas into the ring and working through them. When the turtle idea was first proposed, it seemed a bit of a stretch, but it eventually turned into one of the studio's favorite pieces of work. The Arnold Agency and VW also announced that it was also one of their favorites.

The concept for the commercial involves a turtle without a shell sitting in a garage waiting room waiting for its number to come up. When it does, the turtle walks through into the next room, where it leans up against a shell/hydraulic lift contraption that has the upper part of its shell mounted on it. The underneath part of the shell is pressed against the turtle's belly, and the two halves are welded together.

Curious Pictures scouted several garages in Queens to get an idea of scale and layout, and it referenced several movies for color schemes and set design. It wanted to give the garage an otherworldy feel, to create an industrial amalgam of gadgets and strange devices. It decided to use a color palette of grays, greens, and yellows.

For the turtle, a doll from a previous job was gutted, and a puppet-maker created an original shell-less turtle. Fabric had to be sourced that had

the right scale and sheen to make it look and feel real. Working from sketches, the puppet-maker spent a week or so hand-sewing the puppet together. For the character of the welder, a GI Joe action figure was dressed in an apron and was given a welding shield and torch.

Meanwhile, work started on building the set. The walls were made out of foam core. The windows, doors, and fan housings were cut out, then painting started. Pictures of gauges from the web were scaled down, cut out of paper and painted. They were glued to the foam core and then on to the painted set. The hydraulic lifts were made out of wood, and the turtle shells were sourced cheaply on the web; the fans were from Chinatown and their housings built out of balsa wood. Everything else on the set was handmade from balsa wood, foam core, or plastic.

A combination of lighting techniques was used to achieve a mix of that fluorescent waiting-room feel and hard light to accent the fans and create fan shadows on the floor. The spot was shot with a Canon 20D digital SLR with the 18-mm–55-mm lens that comes with the package.

The shot that involved tracking the turtle as it gets up and walks into the next room proved to be the most tricky. However, the problem was soon solved: in the basement of the Curious Pictures building there was an old-school hand-crank animation rail, about 10 ft (3 m) long with a threaded crank running down the center on which a camera could be mounted. Eight full cranks were needed to move the camera just 1 in. (3 cm). After some practice, the tracking move was shot. The footage was cut by turning the image sequences into uncompressed QuickTimes,

importing them into Final Cut Pro and editing them. Finally, the sound design and music were added. All told, the fifteen-second spot took about a month to complete.

TOOLS
Apple Final Cut Pro

CREDITS
Direction: Ugly Pictures
Animation: Rohitash Rao, Abraham Spear, Taylor Jordan, Camilla Wycoco
Puppet-maker: Camilla Wycoco
Music/Sound Design: Josh Kirsch/ Kirsch Electric

PROFILE

Beatriz Helena Ramos is the founder of Dancing Diablo Studio, an innovative animation studio with offices in New York and Caracas, Venezuela. As creative director, Ramos is responsible for the studio's characteristic fresh style. Ramos has directed numerous animated pieces for TV, and supervises a staff of approximately fifteen artists and other employees. Dancing Diablo's clients include Fuse, NOGGIN, Oxygen, JWT, Saatchi & Saatchi, and Ogilvy & Mather. Ramos's illustrations have appeared in such publications as the *New York Times* and *Penthouse*, and her paintings have been exhibited in several New York galleries.

STEPS TO CREATION

Ramos tends toward fantastical concepts and magical worlds, so to execute a realistic concept such as the health advice in *Get Up and Grow*, she had to find the magic in the message. Since Ramos has a lot of experience doing children's

illustrations, she decided to design the animation in the style of a magical moving painting. To make it less realistic, she eliminated the perspective completely and made it look totally two-dimensional. She also made the textures of the brushstrokes very obvious and the color combination unusual and whimsical.

Once Ramos had come up with a concept that she liked, her studio worked out a style frame to show how the girl and her world were going to look. From there, boards were made to define how the story was going to

be told. Next, a simple animatic was constructed to set the time and rhythm of the piece. All the designs were done traditionally, with acrylic paint and color pencils. The piece was composed and animated in After Effects, except for the girl's arms and legs, which were animated traditionally frame by frame.

TOOLS
Acrylic paint and color pencils, Adobe After Effects, Adobe Photoshop

CREDITS
Directors: Beatriz Helena Ramos, Peter Sluszka
Art Director: Beatriz Helena Ramos
Producer: Vicky Smith
Animation: Ivan Abel

DANCING DIABLO STUDIO
TITLE: JETBLUE
CLIENT: JETBLUE
FORMAT: TV COMMERCIAL

STEPS TO CREATION

The airline JetBlue gave Dancing Diablo Studio twenty stories to develop into style frames, each with a different design style and type of animation. Each of the artists in the studio proposed at least one style, and JetBlue picked this particular one.

The main challenge was to take a metaphorical rather than a literal approach, so a simple type of drawing was used. Mixing paper textures with photographic elements focused attention on the character animations rather than the background. Initially, the studio applied the style to the story's two main characters, testing and manipulating the original video to make a collage of the faces combined with some simple 2D animated cycles.

Once the design was finalized, the storyboards and animatics were finished. A sound designer added the audio track, which further enhanced the atmosphere. All graphics were composited in After Effects, and stop-motion animation was used to depict the snowstorm.

TOOLS
Adobe After Effects, Adobe Photoshop, Autodesk Combustion

CREDITS
Director: Adriana Genel
Producer: Diego Sánchez
2D Animation: Juan Riera, Deryck Morales, Vanessa Rodriguez, Adriana Genel
Stop-motion Animation/Compositing: Alejandro Armas
Music/Sound Design: Andy Green, Alan Friedman

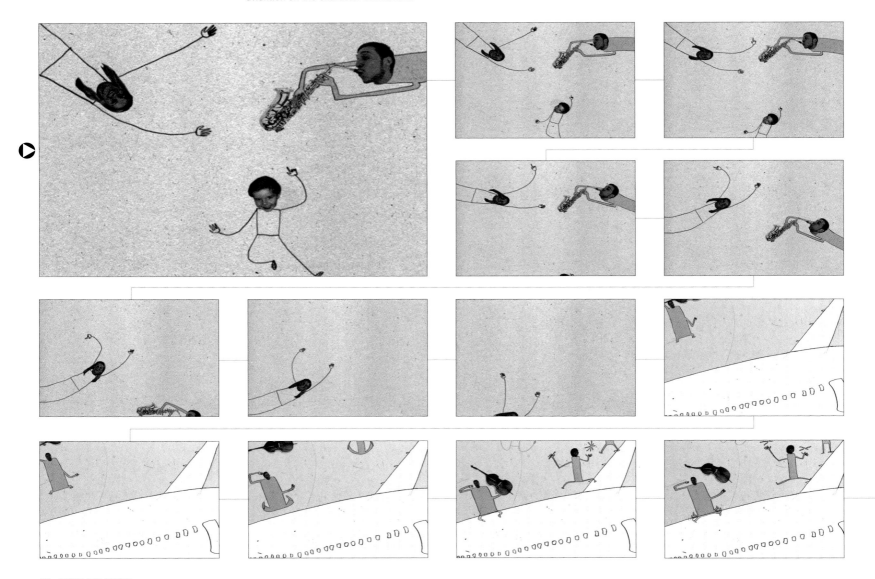

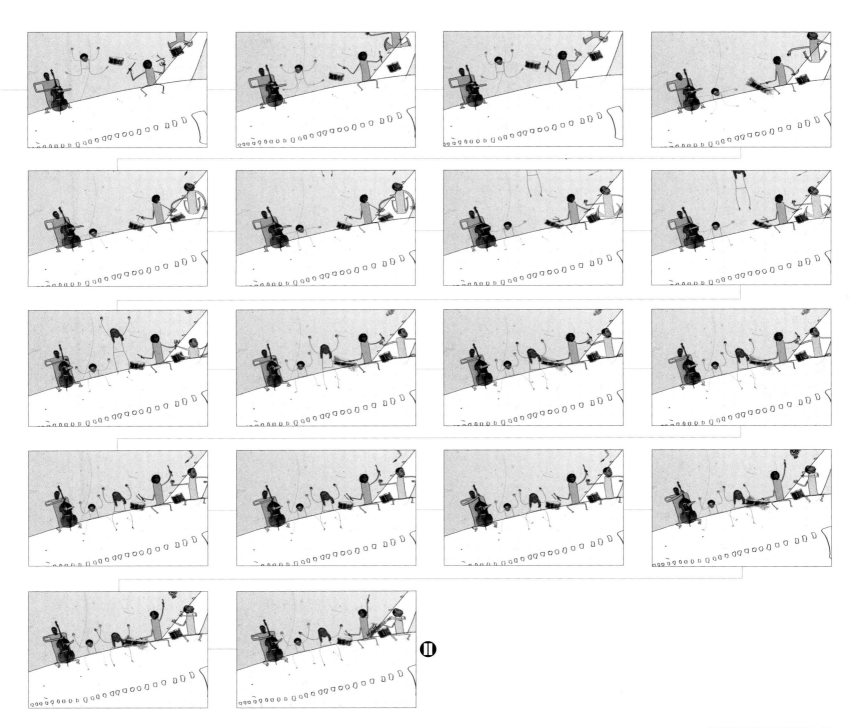

DIGITAL KITCHEN
USA
TITLE: 2006 SUNDANCE FILM
FESTIVAL BUMPERS
CLIENT: SUNDANCE
FORMAT: SHORT FILMS

PROFILE

In 1995, the Digital Kitchen broadcast production company was founded to cultivate and advance broader experimentation and creativity in full-motion electronic media, leveraged with an uncommon faculty for strategic brand marketing. The company now has studios in Seattle, Chicago, and New York, and provides development, design, and production for advertising, TV entertainment, and feature films. Focusing on collaborative authorship, Digital Kitchen uses live-action production, motion graphics, 3D design, and visual effects to create for such clients as AT&T, Coca-Cola, Microsoft, HBO, Nike, NBC, and Infinity.

STEPS TO CREATION

Digital Kitchen was charged with bringing the story of Icarus to life, using artwork provided by Adams Morioka, the festival branding designers. Digital Kitchen had to illustrate four different interpretations of the story, which were going to be used as bumpers in the festival film programs.

Because of budget constraints, the live-action portion of the production needed to be as simple as possible. Before a single frame of celluloid was burned, working animatics were created for each story, and were used to map imagery selection, timing, and the basic story arc. Preparation for the live action followed. The low budget dictated a minimal lighting and camera package and the need for strict economy. Every crew member had to perform multiple tasks.

Three of the four pieces had some live action, and this was shot in a single day on 35-mm film. Small vignettes were created to act as the miniature sets. One of the pieces, *Precipice*, was created in a single take; a jib arm was used to achieve a motion-control-like journey through its set. The paper cutouts and hands were also shot for the *Flame Out* story, and the book used in *Pop-Up* was shot practically on

a C-stand as a plate. *The Fall* had no live-action component and was done entirely in After Effects.

No color correction was done to the film, because it was transferred as a best light by a Seattle colorist. From there it went straight to postproduction. It took four weeks to complete all four films.

TOOLS
Adobe After Effects, Adobe Illustrator, Adobe Photoshop, SoftimageXSI

CREDITS
Creative Director: Matt Mulder
VFX Director: Dade Orgeron
Producers: Don McNeill, Cynthia Biamon, Wendy McCarty
Design: Ryan Gagnier, Thai Tran, Dan Brown, Colin Day, Lindsay Daniels, Rama Allen
3D Animation: Brian Demong, Cody Cobb

DIGITAL KITCHEN
TITLE: GET IT TOGETHER
CLIENT: COCA-COLA
FORMAT: TV COMMERCIAL

STEPS TO CREATION

What does the taste of Coca-Cola look like? Relying on inventive problem-solving and experimental design techniques, Digital Kitchen developed a complete "micro world", in which the visible flavor essences blend and swirl together. 3D elements combine with live-action footage, including the injection of dense liquid pigment into water, which is shot at 1000 fps, to give the spot a luscious, silky texture. The graphics, meanwhile, respond to the sexy overtones and rhythms of the two "flavor voices:" the inimitable Barry White, and Cree Summer.

For the Cherry Coke concept, the designers imagined a world in which the two flavors collide and blend, after which they created photoreal interpretations of those concepts. The project combined the live action of the "sexy" pour with 3D movement perspective through the bubbles and into the glass.

TOOLS
Adobe After Effects, Adobe Photoshop, Autodesk Maya, Avid Media Composer

CREDITS
Director: Eric Anderson
Producers: Colin Davis, Mark Bashore
Design: Erin Sarofsky, Anthony Vitagliano, Shangyu Yin
3D Animation: Linas Jodwalis, Kirk Shintani
Editor: Andrew Maggio

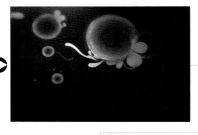 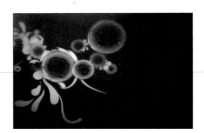  

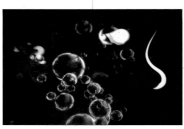 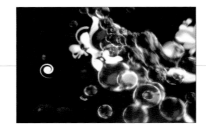  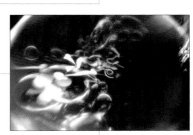

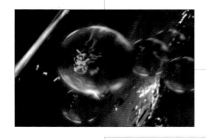 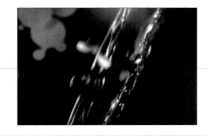  

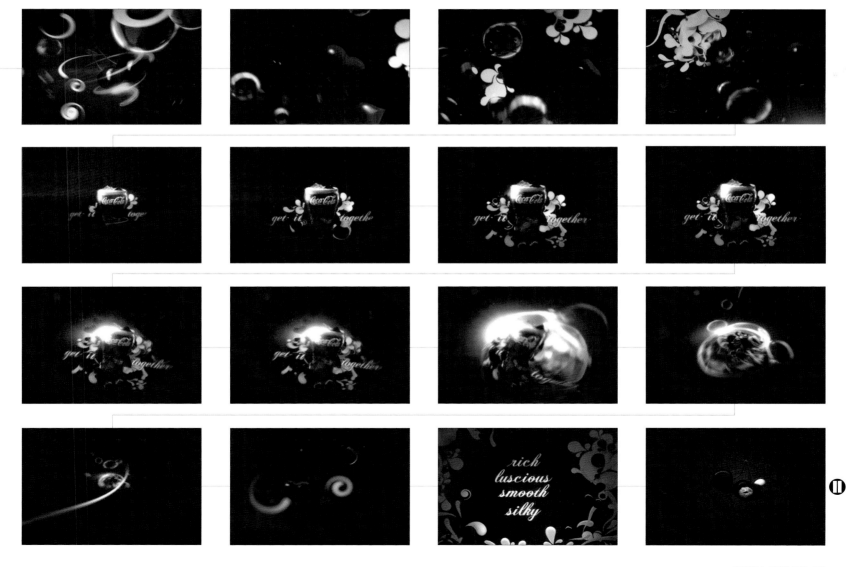

JORDIE DOUBT
SWITZERLAND
TITLE: BOBBY
CLIENT: PERSONAL PROJECT
FORMAT: SHORT FILM

PROFILE

Jordie Doubt got his start in animation in 2002 with the twelve-month intensive 2D program at Vancouver Film School. After graduation, he moved to Solothurn, Switzerland, where he began working at Swamp animation film studio.

In 2005, Jordie won third place in the Bildwurf Minimotion awards with *War*. While at Swamp, he joined forces with four other animators to win the first Talent Screen contest in Zurich, with the stop-motion film *Bobby*.

STEPS TO CREATION

Bobby was created by Doubt and four other animators; all of them were working at Swamp on unrelated projects. The process started when one of them heard of a contest taking place in Zurich. It involved creating a film in two days, on a theme yet to be announced. Most of the participants were live-action filmmakers. The Swamp group's was the only entry to use stop-motion.

Before the group had been given the theme, they bought supplies, mainly

of Styrofoam balls, pipe cleaners, and kinked straws, and experimented with designs for different characters to see how they could be animated. They also tested artwork for the backgrounds, so when they heard the theme, "Laughing and Cleaning," they already had a head start.

The group immediately started brainstorming. After a couple of hours and a few extremely ambitious ideas, they settled on a simple scenario involving two main characters and one big gag. *Bobby* relied on apathetic characters and the element of surprise.

The group quickly created some very rough storyboards. The backgrounds, which were made using black ballpoint pens and pastels on cardboard, were cut out to provide a contrast to the Styrofoam characters.

The two dogs—one for before the incident at the heart of the film, and one for afterward—were made from small mops, which worked out perfectly for the fur. For the man, a groundskeeper, the group made a selection of different heads with different expressions.

After the characters were built, a stage was set and lit, and the various

camera positions composed. Then everyone in the group worked in shifts to animate the rough storyboard using LunchBox—a stop-motion recording device that captures frames straight on to a digital video cassette. When the animation was done, voice-overs were recorded with Adobe Audition, and the film was composited in After Effects. The film was delivered with four minutes to spare.

TOOLS
Adobe After Effects, Adobe Audition, Animationtoolworks LunchBox DV, ballpoint pens and pastels on cardboard

CREDITS
Directors/Producers/Animators: Jordie Doubt, Eva Rust, Sven Rohler, Gaby Schüler, Stefan Holaus

EYEBALLNYC
USA
TITLE: COMEDY CENTRAL BRANDING PACKAGE
CLIENT: COMEDY CENTRAL
FORMAT: NETWORK ID

PROFILE

For Limore Shur, creative director, founder, and owner of EyeballNYC, the creative process is a balance between instinct and reference. For most of his creative ideas, he first looks inside himself and then refers to existing work to help communicate them.

STEPS TO CREATION

EyeballNYC wanted the Comedy Central logo to look as if it had been painted by street artists. The idea was to make abstract elements look as if they were living in an organic and textural world. The designers and animators used different media to build lush and dynamic worlds. The moving elements were animated in the manner of leaves growing on a vine, or ink spreading on paper. Special fonts were designed that were chunky, odd, bold, and aggressive-looking. They were animated to look as if they had been filmed using stop-motion to make the typography seem like a living element. Several strange creatures and compositions developed out of the process.

TOOLS
Adobe After Effects, Adobe Illustrator, Adobe Photoshop

CREDITS
Directors: Limore Shur, Julian Bevan
Producers: Mike Eastwood, Beth Vogt
Design: Carlo Vega, Stuart Simms
Illustration: Ghazia Jalal
Animation: Brian Sensebe, Eric Bauer, Federico Saenz

EYEBALLNYC
TITLE: FOURTH OF JULY
HOLIDAY ID
CLIENT: COMEDY CENTRAL
FORMAT: NETWORK ID

PROFILE

EyeballNYC's creative director, Limor Shur, believes that the creative person relies on depth, composition, and labor. Depth can be found in layers of paint, or in three-dimensional renderings; composition is the balance of information and negative space; labor is the artist/designer's commitment to the message. The successful combination of these qualities has helped award-winning EyeballNYC develop a reputation as an industry groundbreaker.

STEPS TO CREATION

Comedy Central needed some original and humorous holiday IDs. Some great mascot costumes helped inspire the idea of characters acting out traditional holiday celebrations. The vignettes almost wrote themselves.

The staff took on the role of actors and everyone got into costume. The shot was done in HD on a large green-screen stage. The "actors" made sure they exaggerated all their actions in order to reinforce the absurdity and humor. In postproduction, the green-screen footage was tracked and all characters were composited into a 3D environment, where many subtle effects were added to ground the characters into their surroundings.

TOOLS
2d3 Boujou, Adobe After Effects, Adobe Photoshop

CREDITS
Credits for *Fourth of July* are the same as for the Comedy Central Branding Package (see opposite).

FILMTECKNARNA
SWEDEN
TITLE: NEVER LIKE THE FIRST TIME!
CLIENT: INDEPENDENT PROJECT
FORMAT: SHORT FILM

PROFILE

The Swedish company FilmTecknarna was founded in 1981 by Lars Ohlson, Stig Bergqvist, and Jonas Odell. The company produces its own animated short films for the Swedish market and award-winning short films, music videos, and TV programming.

Odell, who created this project, specializes in films combining live action and other techniques, such as cel animation, clay animation, 2D and 3D computer graphics, and cutouts. Odell has also directed music videos for such bands as Franz Ferdinand, Erasure, and U2.

STEPS TO CREATION

Through the use of documentary material, *Never Like the First Time!* explores the issue of how people lose their virginity. Four people describe their experiences. Their stories, presented in four different "chapters," include comedy and tragedy, and the subjects display such emotions as nostalgia, embarrassment, and even horror.

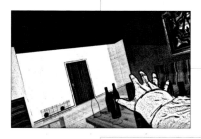   

When Odell selected and edited the interviews he had to think as a scriptwriter but at the same time stay true to the stories. Each interview provided a couple of hours of raw material, and needed to be edited down to a three- to four-minute spot. After doing that, Odell put the spots into a sequence that gave the film an overall narrative structure.

Odell used a different animation technique for each chapter to help illustrate the individual tone of each story, and this resulted in a completely different style for each segment.

The second story, for example, played out in a very schematic way. Focusing on a couple who had met every Saturday for more than a year and had taken small steps toward intimacy each time, leading to that first experience, Odell selected a visually stylized approach reminiscent of airline safety leaflets. To capture both the couple's tenderness and awkwardness, scenes were shot with actors. The actors' movements were then rotoscoped into the stylized drawings of the film, thus allowing the piece to retain the detail and idiosyncrasies of human movement.

By contrast, the third story (shown here) was very dark, and would not have suited anything that remotely resembled cartoon animation. Although actors were also used in this segment, this time they were incorporated into a raw graphic style that helped create feelings of distress and intoxication.

TOOLS
Adobe After Effects

CREDITS
Director/Design/Editor: Jonas Odell
Producer: Susanne Granlöf
Animation: Per Helin, Stefan Ljungberg, Jonas Odell, Arvid Steen, Aron Hagerman, Riina Kütt, Audrone Brasiskyte, Neringa Rackyte

LORENZO FONDA
ITALY
TITLE: FILM FESTIVAL TRAILER
CLIENT: INDEPENDENT FILM FESTIVAL
OF BOSTON
FORMAT: FILM FESTIVAL TRAILER

PROFILE

Lorenzo Fonda, who was twenty-six years old in 2007, was born and raised in Italy; he currently lives in Milan. After a high school education, he started work as a freelance animator. He won a one-year scholarship at Fabrica, the Benetton research center on communication, after which he signed with Mercurio Films, an Italian production company. Since then, Fonda has worked for such clients as Nike, MTV, Paramount Comedy, Sundek, and Morr Music.

STEPS TO CREATION

When the Independent Film Festival of Boston asked Fonda to create a trailer for the event, he visualized the way in which falling dominoes run like film. Fonda asked his father, a physics researcher, to create an interactive data sheet to calculate all the factors he would need to control in order to capture that effect.

Fonda printed on to paper the frames of a short film he'd shot in Milan, and stuck them on rectangular pieces of wood (his "dominoes"). For the first attempt at filming the row of falling

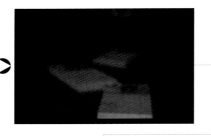
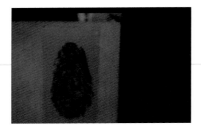
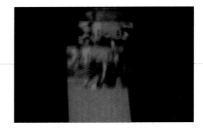
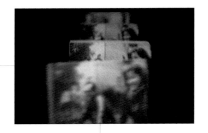

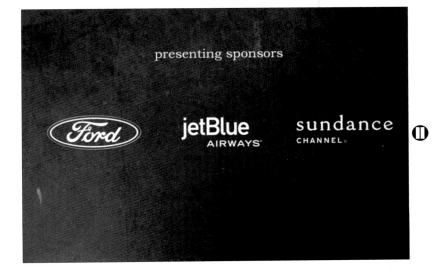

dominoes, the production team plugged a 16-mm camera into a motor and put it on tracks so that it would move at a uniform speed. They discovered that the dominoes fell at different speeds in different parts of the course, however, causing the camera either to crash into the dominoes or to lose focus when the dominoes raced ahead. The camera was unplugged from the motor and pulled by hand instead, and the camera operator had to keep the camera at the right distance. It took the team twelve attempts before they got the right shot.

TOOLS
Adobe After Effects, Adobe Photoshop, Adobe Premiere

CREDITS
Director: Lorenzo Fonda
Director of Photography: Esposito & Chiarello
Physics/Kinetic Research: Sergio Fonda

LORENZO FONDA
TITLE: SKIP THE WINTER
CLIENT: SUNDEK/JWT
FORMAT: WEB CARTOON

STEPS TO CREATION

Originally, the agency JWT wanted an animated twenty-second TV commercial for the Sundek swimwear/surf company. Lorenzo Fonda created two spots for the "Skip the Winter" campaign, an animated TV commercial and a web version. The work turned into a three-minute short animation for the Internet, and the message was: winter is bad and it's best to skip it. Fonda and his illustrator, Sergi Sanchez, were given total creative freedom, and JWT told them to have fun.

Fonda decided to keep the animation style simple so that it would be possible to add and modify scenes quickly. Animation was started without a storyboard or a script, and scenes and situations were improvised.

TOOLS
Adobe After Effects, Adobe Premiere, Macromedia Flash

CREDITS
Director/Animation: Lorenzo Fonda
Illustration: Sergi Sanchez

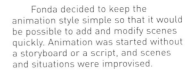

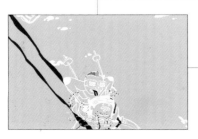

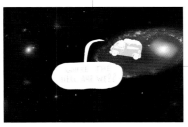

FOREIGN OFFICE
UK
TITLE: MRS HENDERSON PRESENTS
CLIENT: THE WEINSTEIN COMPANY/
PATHÉ PICTURES INTERNATIONAL/
BBC FILMS
FORMAT: TITLE SEQUENCE

PROFILE

London-based Foreign Office is a multinational collective of directors, animators, and designers: Matteo Manzini, Fredrik Nordbeck, and Sonia Ortiz Alcón from Italy, Sweden, and Spain respectively. The company focuses on motion graphics for television and film.

Founded in 1997 under the name 4k, Foreign Office has evolved from being immersed purely in web and print design to producing animation, videos, and IDs for such diverse clients as Philippe Starck, PlayStation, Warner Music Group, Sony, MTV, and Motorola.

STEPS TO CREATION

Director Stephen Frears wanted more than just a title sequence for his film *Mrs Henderson Presents*; he wanted something that would function as a visual representation of the 1930s and set the mood for the story that was about to unfold. As a further challenge, the three-minute animated title sequence had to be delivered to film resolution in just six weeks. Fortunately, a beautiful piece of original music, which had already been composed and mastered for the sequence, offered an excellent starting point.

The soundtrack was set against a timeline and divided accordingly. The amount of screentime allocated to each name was agreed beforehand, and each name had its own theme. Final delivery was at 24 fps (the frame rate of film as opposed to TV broadcast, which is 25 fps or 29.97 fps, depending on the country).

The team brainstormed to determine the visual flow and continuity of the sequence, and a style of animated moving illustrations was agreed upon. Visual stills were generated and gleaned from various sources, and the style for the illustrations was defined.

Foreign Office's lead animator and creative director produced the artwork, and then handed it over to traditional animators, inbetweeners, and digital colorists. Penciled sequences were scanned and line-tested against the music and, once approved, were cleaned up and rescanned at high resolution. Since the final delivery was to film, the average file size was several times larger than that of standard resolution for broadcast television.

Each image was taken individually through Photoshop for digital ink and paint. For the final sequence, Tiff-image strings were imported into After Effects, along with such other elements as 3D and stock-film footage. The 3D artist was given specific timings for each of the key pieces. The main curtain at the beginning of the sequence is a treated piece of stock footage bought for the project, and then flat-graded to look as though it were generated via animation. All other cloth sequences, including the final curtain, were created in Maya.

The final After Effects project was output as a long string of Tiffs, taken to a telecine facility for grading and color correction, and transferred to film negative.

TOOLS
Adobe After Effects, Adobe Photoshop, Autodesk Maya, Macromedia Flash, pencil and paper, Wacom tablet

CREDITS
Title Sequence Direction/Creative Direction: Foreign Office
Lead Animation: Matteo Manzini
Animation: Jill Brooks, Nicolette van Gendt
Music: George Fenton

FOREIGN OFFICE
TITLE: NICKELODEON CRUNCH
CLIENT: NICKELODEON
FORMAT: TITLE SEQUENCE

STEPS TO CREATION

Nickelodeon required a series of four animated graphics to be integrated with live footage. Since the budget was low, Foreign Office needed to find an economical technique.

The theme was "kids' breakfast," and the story—a pair of spectacles offering a view into a new and crazy world—had already been written. Along with a generic opening scene, the shots featuring the characters of Grandma, Dad, and the dog had already been filmed. Edited together, using various techniques, these were used to create four different footage segments. The look was intended to be lively, messy, scruffy, colorful, garish, and bright.

A sense of depth was achieved by creating a multilayered world of two-dimensional elements. These were reconstituted within After Effects, using fly-bys and animated sprites, each with their own set of camera distortions or rotations.

The live footage was supplied as high-resolution QuickTime. It needed to be in the highest resolution possible for accurate rotoscoping (trace animating).

Rotoscoping over the live footage was used only for the short moments of transition between reality and fantasy.

The backgrounds were personal photographs that had been donated by the staff. They were painted over in a semitransparent wash of bright colors. The traffic signs and text elements peppering the landscape all contain catchphrases from the show. The idea was to introduce into the sequence many fast, humorous elements that would add to the overall feel of each spot.

The cityscapes were a series of rapidly scribbled pen-and-ink drawings

that were scanned and colored in Photoshop. The Rocket Dog was digitally animated via a Wacom tablet, first as key frames, and later tweened before color was added. The Jumping Dog is one of a few, very short sequences in which the live action was taken as a direct reference and animation rotoscoped over it.

To give the impression of the viewer seeing through the lenses of a pair of spectacles, the animation was masked (cut out) to match the movement of the spectacles precisely. The masks themselves were moved within After Effects. Later, a distortion filter was placed over the individual graphic TGA (or targa files).

The closing shots of the television on the head of the main character are a good example of tracking. The TV itself is a 2D element created in Photoshop, imported, and later tracked in After Effects to follow the actor. Many of the graphic elements placed on top of the original footage had to be tracked in the shot to follow the live-action camera.

The graphic elements from the final After Effects projects were exported as targa files with traveling mattes, to be composited later.

TOOLS
Adobe After Effects, Adobe Photoshop, Macromedia Flash, pen and ink, Wacom tablet

CREDITS
Director: Akin Akinsiku
Design/Animation: Foreign Office

FREESTYLE COLLECTIVE
USA
TITLE: FUEL CHEMISTRY
CLIENT: FUEL TV
FORMAT: NETWORK ID

PROFILE

Freestyle Collective is a collaborative concept and design studio that has its headquarters in New York City's Flatiron district. Specializing in exploratory and experimental design and production, the company is recognized for its unique artistic sensibility. It delivers creative advertising, promotion, and content for a range of commercial, broadcast, and corporate clients worldwide.

Great design doesn't just grab your attention; it takes hold of your imagination. Freestyle aims to do just that. The illustrators, photographers, painters, filmmakers, collectors, curators, and writers who populate the creative shop are storytellers bringing the client's vision to life.

STEPS TO CREATION

The company's creative process always begins with a brainstorming session to generate ideas and stories. In this case, the team came up with a concept that revolved around a cast of hand-drawn mutant creatures that come to life in a

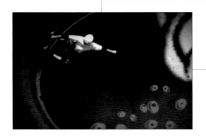

lab after working hours. The creatures have extreme-sport superpowers—skateboarding, BMX freestyling, and so on. The overall tone of the piece was to be strange and eerie, yet nostalgic and whimsical.

Preliminary sketches were made with pen and paper. A short narrative and storyboard were created after the ideas and characters had been fleshed out. The sequence finished with the Fuel TV endtag.

The illustrations were drawn on a sketchpad, after which they were scanned and prepared in Photoshop for animation in After Effects. A few of the characters were put into motion using cel animation. Meanwhile, live-action footage of real skaters and bikers was rotoscoped. Once this was done, the cel animation, rotoscoped footage, and 2D animation were all composited using After Effects.

TOOLS
Adobe After Effects, Adobe Illustrator, Adobe Photoshop, Apple Commotion Pro, pen and paper

CREDITS
Creative Director: Hoon Chong
Executive Producer: Elizabeth Kiehner
Senior Producer: Javier Gonzalez
Design/Illustration: Hoon Chong, Simon Benjamin, Devon Clark
Animation: Simon Benjamin

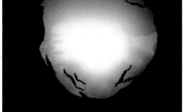

FREESTYLE COLLECTIVE
TITLE: JETBLUE
CLIENT: JETBLUE/JWT
FORMAT: TV COMMERCIAL

STEPS TO CREATION

In this thirty-second commercial for the JetBlue airline, Freestyle Collective used low-tech, handmade cutouts and playful animation to give the story of "ordinary customer" Brad Lampkin a genuine, believable feel.

The campaign is based on the real-life stories of customers. The airline and the agency JWT set up story booths in eight US cities in which people could record stories about flying with JetBlue. Freestyle Collective and other cutting-edge agencies used the audio recordings, and sometimes footage, to create slightly surreal and entertaining commercials.

For Brad's character, designers applied many different kinds of fabric to the illustrations. The multiple textures created a vivid, fantastic world that not only grabs the audience through the colors and layers but also suggests a warm experience. The illustrations are reminiscent of a children's pop-up book and impart a fairy-tale-like feel to the ad.

The designers employed traditional animation techniques and used After Effects for the compositing and animation.

TOOLS
Adobe After Effects

CREDITS
Creative Director: Hoon Chong
Executive Producer: Elizabeth Kiehner
Senior Producer: Javier Gonzalez
Design/Illustration/Animation: Keng-Ming Liu

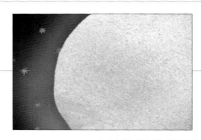

Sincerely,

jetBlue
AIRWAYS

FREESTYLE COLLECTIVE
TITLE: ZOO ROOM
CLIENT: RESISTOR GALLERY
FORMAT: SHORT FILM

STEPS TO CREATION

Toronto's Resistor Gallery invited thirty design studios from around the world to submit exhibits as part of a global fundraiser for the World Wildlife Fund (WWF). The brief was to create films based on the phrase "Zoo room: a room with a zoo." Pieces could feature any type of real or man-made animal in a type of confined space. The works were to be shown on monitors in the gallery, and all the proceeds from the exhibition were to be donated to the WWF.

Freestyle Collective's cofounder and creative director, Victor Newman, has always loved science fiction. He and his team decided to make a piece about an alien poacher spaceship visiting a strange planet and kidnapping exotic life forms. They allowed themselves three weeks to complete the project.

After a period of research, looking at planet surfaces, animal physiology, and plant life, the team drew up some storyboards. They decided to animate the piece in 3D, using Maya. The team consisted of four people, between whom they split the tasks of constructing the

environment, animating the characters, building the spacecraft, and compositing, using After Effects; they all shared the responsibility for texturing and lighting.

During the motion-test phase, the team collaborated with the audio house Tonal, which composed the sound design.

TOOLS
Adobe After Effects, Adobe Illustrator, Adobe Photoshop, Autodesk Maya

CREDITS
Direction/Animation: Freestyle Collective
Sound Design: Tonal

FUEL
USA
TITLE: INKED
CLIENT: FOX/A&E
FORMAT: TITLE SEQUENCE

PROFILE

The Fuel design company was established in 1995, and has offices in New York and Los Angeles. The internationally recognized, Emmy Award-winning firm specializes in broadcast television, advertising, and film, and its expertise includes conceptual design, 2D and 3D animation, font construction, live-action direction, digital photography, illustration, CG modeling, and offline editing.

While Fuel is well known for motion graphics, it also boasts a strong tradition of live-action production. With complete in-house editorial, Fuel can cater to the needs of every project.

STEPS TO CREATION

For a TV show about a real-life Las Vegas tattoo parlor and its clients, an obvious design choice for the title sequence was the exploration of tattoo art. However, the tone and attitude of the animation—the lively camera movement—almost took care of themselves in matching the in-your-face attitude of the main characters.

All the live action was shot on film, but the camera movements were created in After Effects. The show's characters were shot either wide or medium, creating a number of options, for the opening.

Creating camera movement exclusively in After Effects gave more flexibility to the animation, but also presented challenges. Whenever a medium shot or close-up was used, part of the body was out of frame and appeared to be missing. For those shots, it was necessary to create body parts to avoid any jarring breaks in the visual flow. Of course, lots of motion blur and fast movement helped mask any shortcomings, while adding to the overall look and feel. More subtle visual cues, such as grit and paint splatters, helped achieve the final effect.

TOOLS
Adobe After Effects, Adobe Illustrator, Adobe Photoshop

CREDITS
Director: Richard Eng
Producers: Janet Arlotta, Aimee Przybylski
Design: Richard Eng, Maria Rapetskaya
Animation: Shell Blevins, Kevin Laui

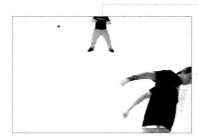

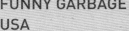

FUNNY GARBAGE
USA
TITLE: BRO RABBIT
CLIENT: DISNEY
FORMAT: TV CARTOON

PROFILE

Funny Garbage is a digital-entertainment studio that specializes in animation and interactive screen design. It was one of the first studios to produce Flash animation in cartoons and games, but quickly grew to develop a full range of animation styles.

Funny Garbage has developed material for Disney and MTV, title sequences for television and film, and broadcast production for Comedy Central and Adult Swim. Other work includes development of animated projects for CNBC correspondent Maria Bartiromo and graphic animation for a variety of interactive websites and projects.

STEPS TO CREATION

Bro Rabbit was a cartoon built around music, and was conceptualized as a hip-hop Bugs Bunny. The concept was turned into a script, which was approved by the producers and then animated in a conventional manner, but the cartoon was inspired by the music and digitally textured paintings.

A script was written and storyboards were drawn directly into Flash using a Wacom LCD tablet. Next, the characters and backgrounds were designed, based on the script and storyboard. Then the soundtrack dialogue was recorded. During the recording, Darrel Hammond, one of the actors, started riffing on the Bro Rabbit character. His take was so perfect that designs and gags were altered to match his performance, and the script, storyboard, and designs had to be tweaked to reflect the new soundtrack.

Backgrounds were drawn in Flash as line drawings, but colored and textured in Photoshop. Character animations were done in Flash and matched to the background and soundtrack using After Effects. All the camera moves were simulated in After Effects.

QuickTime movies were exported for client review each time an adjustment was made to the design, the video, or the soundtrack. The final sound mix was added to the video using Pro Tools.

TOOLS
Adobe After Effects, Adobe Photoshop, Digidesign Pro Tools, Macromedia Flash, Wacom tablet

CREDITS
Director/Writer/Storyboard Artist: Mark Marek
Art Director: Chris Capuozzo
Producers: Kristin Ellington, John Carlin, Susanna Graves
Character Design: Todd James
Animation: Matt Laverty, Dave Redl
Background Artists: Rick Farr, Chris Capuozzo
Music: Andres Levin

FUNNY GARBAGE
TITLE: RAPTOONS
CLIENT: MTV
FORMAT: TV CARTOON

STEPS TO CREATION

The first *Raptoons* was created by Todd James, who was inspired by the comedy of Rudy Ray Moore, and animated to a Thirstin Howell rap song. It was used as a springboard for the final *Raptoons* cartoon, in which gags were beefed up and elements were further developed by the Funny Garbage team.

After a rough script had been written, the soundtrack dialogue was recorded and imported into Flash so the editing could be done on the timeline. Animation was drawn directly into Flash using a Wacom tablet. The soundtrack, artwork, animation, and timing were constantly tweaked and reworked as the project evolved into its final form. With each new version, a video was exported for review.

Final music, sound effects, and mixing were done in Pro Tools, matching the video. The soundtrack was re-edited, using the higher-resolution original sound files rather than the low-res files that had been used in Flash.

TOOLS
Digidesign Pro Tools, Macromedia Flash, Wacom tablet

CREDITS
Director: Mark Marek
Art Directors: Chris Capuozzo, Peter Girardi, Todd James
Producers: Kristin Ellington, John Carlin, Susanna Graves
Storyboard/Character Design: Todd James
Animation: George Lowery, Todd James, Jason Sawtelle, Dave Redl
Background Artists: Rick Farr, Chris Capuozzo

FUNNY GARBAGE
TITLE: PINK DONKEY
CLIENT: CARTOON NETWORK
FORMAT: WEB CARTOON

STEPS TO CREATION

The web cartoon *Pink Donkey* was an experiment for Funny Garbage. It involved animating the work of illustrator Gary Panter as an online series, while trying to conserve the hand-painted feel of his drawings.

First, Panter's illustrations were reworked into a more traditional storyboard, and the soundtrack dialogue was recorded. Character and background elements were drawn and inked on paper and then scanned into Photoshop to be touched up. The files were converted into vector art in Streamline. The artwork was colored and tweaked further in Illustrator. The vector artwork was imported and assembled in Flash. The soundtrack was imported partly into Flash in order that the editing could be done directly on the timeline. Final music, sound effects, and mixing were also done in Flash.

TOOLS

Adobe Illustrator, Adobe Photoshop, Adobe Streamline, Macromedia Flash, pencil and paper

CREDITS

Director: Ric Heitzman
Art Director: Chris Capuozzo
Producers: Kristin Ellington, John Carlin, Denise Rotina, Susanna Graves
Concept Creator/Writer: Gary Panter
Animation: Devin Flynn, Mark Marek, Dave Redl
Music/Sound Effects: Jay Cotton

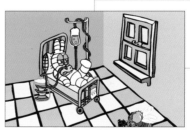

SOPHIE GATEAU
FRANCE
TITLE: FRENCH KISS
CLIENT: FASCINESHION.COM
FORMAT: WEB FEATURE

PROFILE

Sophie Gateau studied architecture and art history in Paris for eight years before focusing on graphic design and film direction at the École Nationale Supérieure des Arts Décoratifs, Paris. Her senior thesis, the short film *I Love Paris*, was shown at the Sonar multimedia festival and the Barcelona film festival, and was featured in the book *A+A: Architecturanimation* (2002).

After graduating, Gateau started work as a CG artist on such feature films as *The Matrix* trilogy, *Alexander*, and *2046*. She is a director at the Paranoid US animation/design studio.

STEPS TO CREATION

Sabine Morandini, the chief editor and creative director of online magazine fascineshion.com, asked Gateau to work on a short animation about lipstick using just minimal elements: ten lipstick tubes and ten multicolored pairs of lips.

The fantasy begins with a world of trees and flowers built out of lipstick

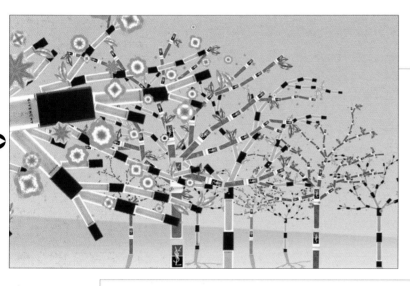

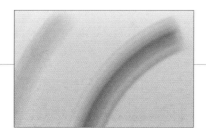

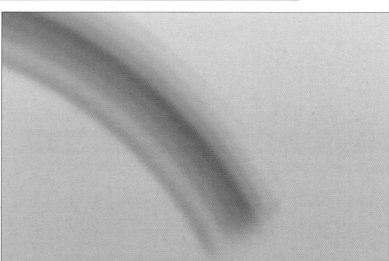

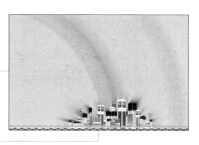

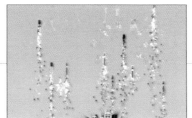

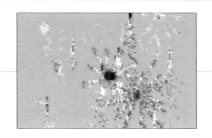

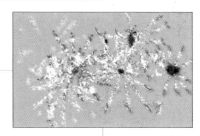

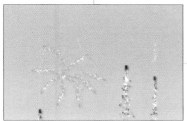

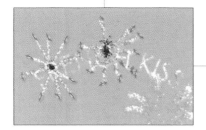

tubes. A rainbow appears, showing the lipstick colors, followed by a city in which the buildings are made up of various lipstick tubes. A lipstick-shaped rocket flies through the sky and explodes into colored fireworks that leave the words "French Kiss" hanging in the air.

The preproduction process started with the visualization of a lipstick world. References were collected, and test elements were drawn on paper, and framed for the camera. Finally, a computer-generated animatic was created to work with the rhythm of the music.

For the actual production, all of those elements were prepared in Photoshop, after which they were animated in After Effects. Once it had been tested in half-resolution, the film was rendered in full resolution.

TOOLS
Adobe After Effects, Adobe Photoshop, pencil and paper

CREDITS
Director: Sophie Gateau
Concept: Sophie Gateau, Sabine Morandini

DARYL GRAHAM
CANADA
TITLE: PLANET SNAK
CLIENT: NABISCO
FORMAT: TV COMMERCIAL

PROFILE

Daryl Graham grew up in southwestern Ontario, Canada, and studied classical animation at Sheridan College. After graduation, he worked for a small studio, based in the Toronto area, that was contracted to Warner Brothers.

Following a stint on feature films, Graham became a commercial director, working in Canada and in the United Kingdom on traditionally hand-drawn jobs for several international clients.

STEPS TO CREATION

For the Planet Snak promotion, the agency supplied a full script, from which Graham and his team developed the storyboard. The storyboard was then filmed and timed to block out the various scenes for the thirty-second spot.

A background was painted in acrylic on panel for each scene. Meanwhile, a 24-fps hand-drawn character animation was created, the animator using the storyboard as a visual guide. The animator used the voice track that

had been prerecorded by the agency as a reference for the character's facial movements.

After the rough animation had been completed and approved by the client, it was cleaned up in black pencil. These black-and-white drawings were scanned into USAnimation, where they were colored and merged with the backgrounds.

From there on, the job went to a postproduction house, where the final sound was added, the color corrected, and some minor compositing effected in Flame.

TOOLS
Acrylic paint on panel, Autodesk Flame, pencil and paper, USAnimation

CREDITS
Directors: Daryl Graham, Chuck Gammage
Producer: Anne Deslauriers
Animation: Daryl Graham, Chuck Gammage, Shannon Penner
FX Animation: Raymond Pang
Background Artists: Clive Powsey, Daryl Graham

THE GROOP
USA
TITLE: AIWAWORLD
CLIENT: AIWA
FORMAT: WEBSITE

PROFILE

Founded in 2001 by Mary Gribbin and Jose Caballer, The Groop collaborates with clients to create dynamic user experiences that help them better communicate, engage, and transact with customers. By combining creativity and flexibility with business and technology experience, The Groop leads clients through the rapidly changing integration of PC, TV, and mobile technologies.

STEPS TO CREATION

Developed in three main sections, the Aiwaworld website featured Aiwamals, Sonics, and Aiwa TV. The first allowed users to combine characters called Aiwamals (Aiwa + Animals), each of which represented one of nine musical genres, such as hip-hop, punk, and pop, into new "hybrid" genres, such as pop/punk. The Sonics section allowed users to view animated characters called Sonics that highlighted the new Aiwa logo and the pronunciation of the brand name

through original songs. The Aiwa TV section contained original pieces by designers Tokyoplastic and Mumbleboy.

Production of Aiwaworld involved forty people working in more than ten disciplines and in four different time zones. The challenge was to create a dynamic and animated interactive experience that used the minimum amount of text-based navigation. This was accomplished by creating an unprecedented audiovisual experience, combining advanced Flash action scripting and a Flash-based 3D engine with detailed character animation and extensive sound design. According to Groop executive creative director, Jose Caballer, "This was as close to producing a film as we can come in an interactive project. Both the pace of production and the breadth of disciplines were staggering."

While the Flash framework was being worked on and the mechanics of the interface were being fine-tuned, a team of designers and animators was creating and animating thirty-nine unique Aiwamal combinations. Meanwhile, a sound-design team was creating the thirty-nine unique permutations of musical genres. A team of designers and animators also worked on the three Aiwa TV animated promos.

TOOLS
Adobe Dimensions, Adobe Illustrator, Adobe Photoshop, Macromedia Dreamweaver, Macromedia Flash

CREDITS
Creative Directors: Tony Davidson, Kim Papworth
Producers: Sharon Tani, Kenji Tanaka, Tony Wong, Frank Mele, Szu Ann Chen
Design: Yiing Fan, Sun An, Paul Hwang, Guy Featherstone, Joshua Trees
Aiwa TV Content Creators: Mumbleboy, Tokyoplastic
Music/Sound Design: Jorge Verdin, Lem Jay Ignacio, Chaz Windus

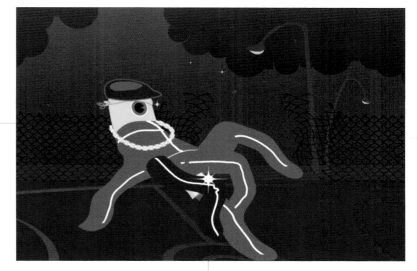

ÖZGÜL GÜRBÜZ
TURKEY
TITLE: LOVE AND MARRIAGE
CLIENT: PERSONAL PROJECT
FORMAT: SHORT FILM

PROFILE

Özgül Gürbüz was born in Eskişehir, Turkey, and graduated with a degree in animation from Anadolu University. After graduation, she became a research assistant and started work on her masters degree. At the end of 2006, Gürbüz resigned from her research post. Since then, she has worked as a 3D-character modeler on a variety of animations and commercials, including such films as *Eti*, *Demirdöküm*, *Arçelik*, and *Ülker-YUPO*. *Love and Marriage*, the short film featured here, is not a commercial work but a personal project. It won the Hamburg Animation Award in 2005, and the AniBOOM Award in 2007.

STEPS TO CREATION

While still at university, Gürbüz developed an interesting theory about love, marriage, and deception. She came to the conclusion that married people often viewed "love" as an obligation. While love was unpredictable and random, marriage seemed to be

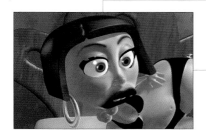

repetitive. Therefore, Gürbüz decided, love and marriage were different and could not possibly coexist.

Gürbüz began to work on a story that explored the institution of marriage. She came up with three characters for the film: a woman, her husband, and a gigolo. For the story to work, the characters needed opposing traits and attitudes. For example, the wife is amorous, while the husband is listless; the husband is sentimental, but the gigolo is coarse. Gürbüz also wanted the characters to have a 'toon style, so she used exaggerated proportion to bring out

their characteristics. After the designs were set, she prepared a model sheet for each character.

Next, Gürbüz created a storyboard and an animatic, working out the camera motions, timing, and animation style. The characters and backgrounds were modeled in Maya. To give the scenes a romantic atmosphere, candles and textures of soft and warm colors were added. All the textures, shadings, and lightings were done in Photoshop. The compositing and the edits on the rendered scenes were completed in After Effects.

TOOLS
Adobe After Effects, Adobe Photoshop, Autodesk Maya

CREDITS
Director/Producer/Animation/Modeling: Özgül Gürbüz
Compositing/Editor: Ajlan Altug

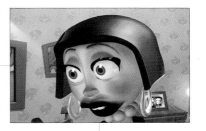

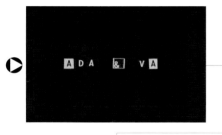

KLARA HAJKOVA
CZECH REPUBLIC
TITLE: ADAM & EVA
CLIENT: ZLÍN FILM COLLEGE
FORMAT: SHORT FILM

PROFILE

Klara Hajkova was born in the Czech Republic in 1982. She studied graphic design and film animation at the Zlín Film College. She completed her first commercial assignment for the Zlín International Film Festival for Children. Hajkova is now a freelance animator, focusing on traditional cutout, hand-drawn animation, but she also works with After Effects and Flash. She has worked on the Czech TV series *Travelers Bob and Bobby*, and in 2006 she directed and animated *Adam & Eva*.

STEPS TO CREATION

Adam & Eva is based on the biblical tale of the first two humans. Adam and Eva are depicted as simple, minimalist, and almost unisex characters.

The storyboard was useful for the camera operator and the sound engineer, but was not used during shooting. This was in keeping with Hajkova's favorite surrealist artist and animator, Jan Svankmajer, who believes that if you need to look at the storyboard more than three times during a shoot, there is something wrong with the film. Hajkova

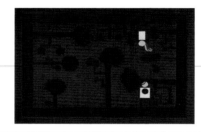

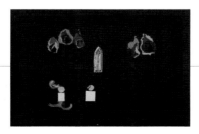

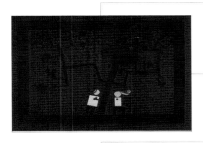   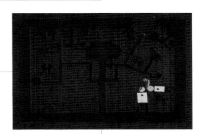

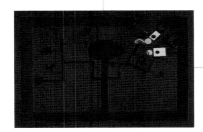  

just played with the animation timing, occasionally adding such unplanned items as the butterflies.

Animation took twenty-seven days, but the screening showed several errors in the animation and the light. Fortunately, editor Jiří Krška was able to recut the film, and sound engineer Ondřej Gášek reworked the music digitally to compensate for all the changes. The result is a miracle.

TOOLS
35-mm studio camera, cutting table, DivX video camera, Cubase, Fruity Loops

CREDITS
Director/Animation: Klara Hajkova
Camera Operator: Laco Kolář
Editor: Jiři Krška
Music: Ondřej Gášek, Markéta Šmejkalová

ANDREAS HYKADE
GERMANY
TITLE: RING OF FIRE
CLIENT: PERSONAL PROJECT
FORMAT: SHORT FILM

PROFILE

Andreas Hykade was born in Germany in 1968. He studied animation at the Staatliche Akademie der Bildenden Künste in Stuttgart. Since then, he has directed, designed, and animated more than eighty commercials, video clips, children's films, TV trailers, and much more. The two short films featured in this book form part of Hykade's "Country Trilogy," which explores his childhood in the countryside; the third film is called *We Lived in Grass.*

STEPS TO CREATION

Ring of Fire is about two cowboys who visit a whore bazaar; one is interested in the flesh, the other, the soul beneath the flesh. Hykade wrote the script and designed the main figures and the set. The people in the whore bazaar were designed from drawings people sent him about their sexual desires.

The film was animated on paper, and each figure had its own dedicated animator in order to help make each character distinct. The artwork was scanned into LightWave—a 3D

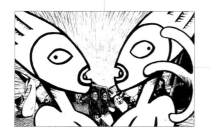

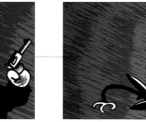

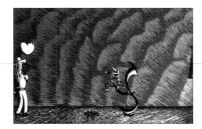

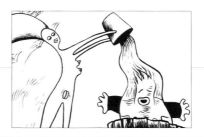

environment—and animated on beat to fit the score. It was finished in 35-mm CinemaScope to evoke the Western feeling.

TOOLS
Ink scratched on cel, NewTek LightWave 3D, pencil and paper

CREDITS
Director/Writer/Design: Andreas Hykade
Technical Director: Michael Wolf
Producer: Michael Jungfleisch/Gambit in coproduction with Studio Film Bilder
Animation: Ged Haney, Jürgen Haas, Anita Ortega, Ralf Bohde, Andreas Hykade
Artwork: Susanne Reinhardt, Natalia Eck, Anna Böck
Music Composition: Steffen Kahles

ANDREAS HYKADE
TITLE: THE RUNT
CLIENT: PERSONAL PROJECT
FORMAT: SHORT FILM

STEPS TO CREATION

When Andreas Hykade was a child, his family bred rabbits for food. After a litter was born, his father and uncle would decide how many rabbits they should keep. His uncle would put the rest of them in a basket and throw them against the wall to kill them.

With those childhood images in mind, Hykade created the story of a little boy who falls in love with the runt of the litter. "Alright," says the uncle. "I'll give you the runt, but you take care of it and you kill it in one year." "Yes,"

says the boy. "I'll take care of it, and I will kill it in one year."

Hykade wrote the script and designed the figures and the set. He polished the animatic until every bit of the storytelling was resolved. The film was animated on paper, and the finished artwork was scanned into a computer. After Effects and Moho were used to create the effects of the changing light and the moving heavens. The score was written after the picture was finished.

TOOLS
Adobe After Effects, Lost Marble Moho, pastels and paper

CREDITS
Director/Writer/Design/Animation: Andreas Hykade
Technical Director: Tobias Pfeiffer
Producer: Thomas Meyer-Hermann/Studio Film Bilder
Artwork: Susanne Reinhardt, Helene Tragesser, Frauke Striegnitz
Music Composition: Ulrich Reuter

  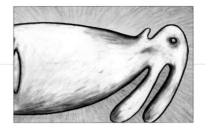 

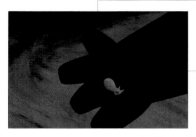   

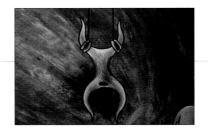

MURRAY JOHN
SOUTH AFRICA
TITLE: THE EIGHTIES MATCHBOX
B-LINE DISASTER
CLIENT: ISLAND RECORDS
FORMAT: TV COMMERCIAL + INTERNET VIRAL

PROFILE

Murray John was born in Krugersdorp, South Africa, and grew up in Johannesburg. After completing his schooling, he studied advertising, graduating in 1994 with a student Clio and Loerie award for his first animation. John then spent eighteen months working as an assistant art director at Young & Rubicam. In 1998, he started working as a runner at London animation production company Bermuda Shorts, and ended up directing, animating, designing, and illustrating.

STEPS TO CREATION

When John first heard The Eighties Matchbox B-Line Disaster, he fell in love with their music. For this commercial advertising a CD by the band, John took themes from the various songs and pieces of the album cover. There wasn't time to perfect the animation (John had only one week to complete the job), so he opted for a strong illustrative style and hoped that it would be enough to carry the piece.

The film starts with the band traveling in a car at fast speed, past some gigantic half-buried skulls. The tops of the skulls flip open and out come some gigantic flying chickens that swallow up the car, which disappears into darkness. The car headlights swirl round at very high speed to form the cover of the band's CD single. This in turn changes into a microphone in the singer's hand, and the whole band is revealed, singing and playing, and synched to the final track.

The idea was to start with the storyboard and limit the animation by using just the frames in After Effects. The twelve-frame storyboard was completed in a day. The characters were all drawn in Illustrator and animated in After Effects. The backgrounds were mostly done in Photoshop and distorted in After Effects. The chickens were colorized photos; no animals were harmed in any way during the making of the film.

TOOLS
Adobe After Effects, Adobe Illustrator, Adobe Photoshop

CREDITS
Director/Design/Animation: Murray John

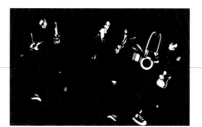

MURRAY JOHN
TITLE: BBC TEENS PROMO
CLIENT: BBC
FORMAT: TV COMMERCIAL

STEPS TO CREATION

Murray John was so excited about doing these designs for the BBC children's channel CBBC that he wanted to go "super-hyper-adrenaline yee-haa" on them. His aim was to create a bold graphic feel with strong colors.

John found it hard making the teenage boy and girl look "cool": in the sketches they kept coming out too thin or too fat, too old, or too young, and so on. John wanted the characters to appear slightly superhuman and to be active, always running and jumping.

The story opens with two teenagers. One whacks the other on the back, and they begin sprinting after each other through a dimly lit parking lot. The scene ends with them flying, Superman-style, into the distance. The background is made up of light and dark pillars with minimal detail in order to create the feeling of an endless, deserted parking lot.

Since time was short, the animations were made looped in order that they could be reused if necessary. Murray drew the character key frames, and an animator created the loop in pencil. The artwork was inked with a

fine-liner and scanned into Photoshop, where the shadows were added, and the artwork was paint-bucketed. From there, everything was imported into After Effects, where the 3D camera movements were added. All the backgrounds were created in After Effects using the 3D camera and lights. The characters were then cut to the beat of a mad track, using split screens to stretch out the loops in an interesting way.

TOOLS
Adobe After Effects, Adobe Photoshop, pencil and paper

CREDITS
Director/Design/Animation: Murray John
Producer: Jade Caffoor
Additional Animation: Eoin Clarke

IGOR KOVALYOV
RUSSIA
TITLE: MILCH
CLIENT: INDEPENDENT COPRODUCTION
FORMAT: SHORT FILM

PROFILE

Igor Kovalyov is an internationally acclaimed filmmaker, designer, animator, and director. His short films *Andrei Svislotsky, Bird in the Window*, and *Flying Nansen* have received numerous awards and garnered accolades from the animation and film community.

Kovalyov was born in Kiev, Ukraine, and was the cofounder of Moscow's Pilot School of Animation. In 1991, he accepted an invitation to work at the Klasky Csupo animation studio in Hollywood. With Norton Virgien, he directed Klasky Csupo's first feature film, *The Rugrats Movie*, and the TV series *Aaahh!!! Real Monsters*.

STEPS TO CREATION

Milch is a fifteen-minute film that tells the story of a boy who discovers love and comes face to face with the mortality of members of his family. The film was based on the conceptual art of Dima Malanitchev, production designer on several of the Rugrats movies. Through a web of oblique detail,

the film attempts to capture the essence of relationships and, perhaps, the very tension of being.

To perfect the film's unique look, multiple tests were run. Three or four key scenes were set up in Toon Boom Opus compositing software. Setup involved digital x-sheeting, and scanning and painting the artwork for these scenes before importing Malanitchev's backgrounds. From there, a full month was spent refining the look and trying to match the feel of Malanitchev's work. In some cases, work on effect lighting,

texturization, and cross-dissolves took several days.

Once the film was in production, a small scanning and painting crew was hired to prepare the sets, while the rest of the team digitally x-sheeted the scenes (there were more than eighty of them). As scenes were scanned and painted, Malanitchev's backgrounds were pulled in to complete the setup. All lighting cues were taken from the backgrounds as shots were built. After a scene was completed, it was forwarded for editing and approval. Some of the more complex

scenes took several sessions to be approved.

Once the core scenes were finished and approved, they were sent to a film recorder and viewed at Deluxe Laboratories to see if the effects worked on film. After many modifications, the effects were ready. This process allowed all parties to have maximum flexibility and input, but it took roughly six months of actual technical directing time to complete the project.

TOOLS
Adobe Photoshop, Avid Media Composer, Toon Boom Opus

CREDITS
Director: Igor Kovalyov
Producers: Gabor Csupo, Arlene Klasky, Genrich Padva
Art/Concept: Dima Malanitchev, Igor Kovalyov
Animation: Chrisdo Stomboliev, Val Konoplev, Evgueni Delioussine
Editors: Igor Kovalyov, Peter Tomaszewicz

LOYALKASPAR
USA
TITLE: PINBACK, "FORTRESS"
CLIENT: TOUCH AND GO RECORDS
FORMAT: MUSIC VIDEO

PROFILE

Recognizing that the process is often more rewarding than the end result is just one of the ways design/production house Loyalkaspar distinguishes itself from the creative herd. Founded in 2003 by directors David Herbruck and Beat Baudenbacher, Loyalkaspar has quickly earned a reputation among advertising creatives and network producers as a hub where daring creative thinking and innovative execution intersect.

Recent Loyalkaspar work includes an international spot for Finnish bank Sampo, web commercials for McCann-Erickson's Microsoft Windows XP campaign, and music videos for Calexico and Pinback.

STEPS TO CREATION

The classic romantic tale of doomed young lovers gets an intriguing and delightful twist in the video for Pinback's "Fortress." Loyalkaspar and codirector Elliot Jokelson tell the tale with great emotion, using primitively drawn stick figures against elaborate

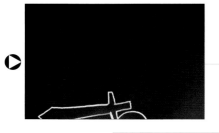

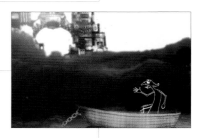

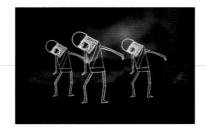

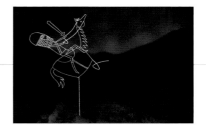

backgrounds. Opening with the scorched earth of a medieval battlefield, *Fortress* reveals a stick-figure prince and princess who were once lovers but are now separated by a bloody war. As they sit grimly behind their respective parapets, their thoughts turn to better days. The lovers' backstory is seen in flashback, against the verdant landscape of a once-vibrant kingdom.

Loyalkaspar strove for the feelings evoked by other tales of the age-old story of star-crossed lovers and warring families, or communities: a little *Romeo and Juliet*, a little "One Tin Soldier," a little *West Side Story*. Since a stick figure's range of emotions is limited, the team combined that simplicity with complex backgrounds to evoke the right mood.

The stick figures were hand-drawn, then retraced in Illustrator. The scenes are a combination of photographs, drawings, and textures. The detailed environments convey a storybook feeling and contrast with the simplicity of the animated line drawings. The project was animated entirely in After Effects.

TOOLS
Adobe After Effects, Adobe Illustrator, Adobe Photoshop, SoftimageXSI

CREDITS
Direction: Loyalkaspar, Elliot Jokelson
Producers: Lindsay Odanza, Jonathan Lia
Design/Illustration/Animation: Beat Baudenbacher, Leah Beeferman, Tavet Gillson, Josh Goodrich, Lauren Hartstone

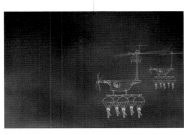
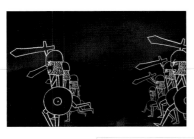
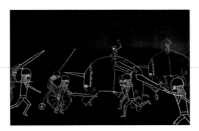

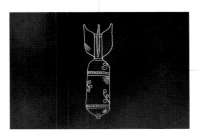

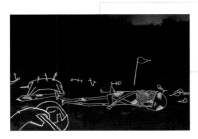

LOYALKASPAR
TITLE: IDEAS INTO ACTION
CLIENT: SAMPO BANK
FORMAT: TV COMMERCIAL

STEPS TO CREATION

In this ad for the Finnish bank Sampo, a nebulous yet vaguely human blue blob floats dejectedly through space against a background of washed-out yellow. In the manner of a fairy tale, a voice-over identifies the lonely blob as "Idea." Floating through a surreal environment of photographic collage, the lonely Idea thinks about watering its flowers, changing a lightbulb, getting a boat to ride, and finding a house in which it can take shelter in a storm. The character cannot act on its ideas,

however, until it meets a four-limbed, headless, and directionless creature named "Action." Able only to run aimlessly in circles until it meets Idea, Action is the yang to Idea's yin.

In a mock slow-mo romance movie moment, the hitherto nebulous blob lands on top of the previously headless creature, uniting Idea and Action, and becoming a single, functioning, autonomous being. A piggybank dramatically transforms into a house, a stick of wood into a rowboat, and a sunlike balloon lights up the house and waters the flowers. In short, Idea and Action live happily ever after.

Loyalkaspar spent the first two weeks of this month-long project fleshing out a multitude of ideas for the all-important Idea character. The agency selected this from twenty or more possibilities presented by the team.

In preproduction, Loyalkaspar spent a good deal of time creating an animation rig to control the character's emotions. An "emotion template," comprising ten to twelve different facial orchestrations, suggested a range of emotions.

The character was created in 3D using Softimage. The backgrounds are

 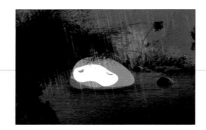  

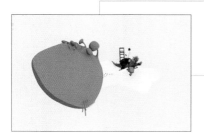   

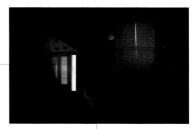

intentionally childish, a simple and crudely animated blend of source photography, illustrations, and vector artwork. The primitive nature of the environments allows the character to emote with such success.

TOOLS
Adobe After Effects, Adobe Illustrator, Adobe Photoshop, SoftimageXSI

CREDITS
Direction: Jakob Ström, Loyalkaspar
Producers: Sarah Grey, Mark Groeschner
Design/Animation/Postproduction: Loyalkaspar

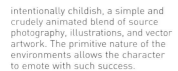

TAKAGI MASAKATSU
JAPAN
TITLE: LIGHT POOL
CLIENT: PERSONAL PROJECT
FORMAT: SHORT FILM

PROFILE

Multimedia artist Takagi Masakatsu describes his work as a collage of sound, music, and video, interpreting classical beauty through new technology. He lives and works in Kyoto, Japan, but has performed and exhibited internationally. In recent years, Masakatsu has mounted solo exhibitions at the Byblos Gallery in Verona, Italy; the Transplant Gallery in New York; the Museum of Contemporary Art in Tokyo; and the Whitechapel Gallery in London, among other places. In 2006, he published a book of his video-arts collection, *Bloomy Girls*.

Masakatsu is a classically trained pianist. He gives public performances, and recordings of his compositions have been released in the United States and Japan.

STEPS TO CREATION

Masakatsu begins each new video work without contemplating or fixing a concept beforehand, but with just a

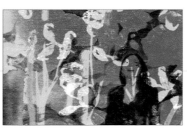

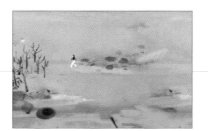

simple item. When he started *Light Pool*, he had been musing on lightning and the vital forces of planet Earth. He developed the notion that people were interconnected via light.

Masakatsu was in Los Angeles when he started *Light Pool*. He had shot footage of girls swimming in a pool, which he kept watching carefully, over and over again before he started work.

Masakatsu never prepares scripts beforehand, but simply starts from the first scene. Once he has that, the work itself "talks" to him, and he follows it to the next scene and its natural conclusion.

For Masakatsu, the process of making a video starts when the material is exported from the digital video into the computer. Once he has everything assembled, he edits without sound, letting the visuals express all they can. After he has edited and arranged the visuals, Masakatsu thinks about sound. His compositions compensate for any shortcomings in the visuals.

It usually takes Masakatsu one to two months to complete a single work.

TOOLS
Adobe After Effects, Apple Final Cut Pro, Apple Logic Pro

CREDITS
Director/Producer/Sound: Takagi Masakatsu

MK12
USA
TITLE: THE HISTORY OF AMERICA
CLIENT: INTERNAL PROJECT
FORMAT: SHORT FILM

PROFILE

Artist collective and design lab MK12 was founded in Kansas City by five art-school fugitives. The five have carved for MK12 a unique niche in the design world, where art, commerce, film, and music happily coexist.

Among its numerous experimental projects, MK12 has completed broadcast and commercial design work for such clients as Diesel, the Sci-Fi Channel, MTV, Cartoon Network, TNT, AXN, and Fox Movie Channel, as well as music videos for Hot Hot Heat and The Faint. MK12's other work includes the experimental films *Untitled 02: Infinity, 4D Softcore Sweaterporn,* and *Ultra Love Ninja,* and trailers for the Resfest film festival.

STEPS TO CREATION

As with much of MK12's experimental work, *The History of America* uses a montage-based approach in which processed live action, 3D environments, and 2D textures coexist to create a single visual approach. Actors were shot

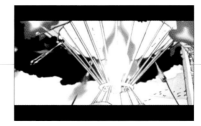

against green screen and inserted into CG environments that ranged from literal representations to abstract designs.

With *The History of America*, the idea was to establish an organic, painterly style for both the live action and the CG environments. To accomplish this, MK12 developed a method of processing live-action footage to mimic the look of the sets. The sets were realized through a combination of scanned paintings and textures, which were modified with 3D 'toon shading tools. Such secondary

effects as smoke and explosions were approached in the same way, often relying on live-action, real-world effects, but also employing 2D and 3D particle systems.

Since *The History of America* is a narrative, short-film project with a heavy live-action component, a huge amount of time was spent in preproduction, tweaking the script, brainstorming, and creating a set of linear storyboards. From there, stylistic mockups were created that served as a template for the overall look of the film. A rough cut was

developed, using the storyboards as live action and animation placeholders. This dictated the length of the animated sequences.

A three-week, live-action green-screen shoot was scheduled, which was cataloged and integrated into the rough cut. Once the rough cut was finished, it was used as an animation template. Rough 3D environments were generated and dropped behind the actors. The live action, texturing, and secondary effects were added after the backdrops were completed.

TOOLS
Adobe After Effects, Adobe Creative Suite, Autodesk Maya, Digidesign Pro Tools

CREDITS
Directors/Producers: Ben Radatz, Jed Carter, Tim Fisher, Shaun Hamontree, Matt Fraction

 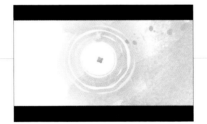 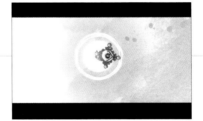 

MOTION THEORY
USA
TITLE: IT CONSOLIDATES
CLIENT: HEWLETT-PACKARD
FORMAT: TV COMMERCIAL

PROFILE

Founded in 2000, Los Angeles-based production company Motion Theory brings together directors, designers, and visual-effects artists in order to create powerful commercials, music videos, and other short projects. With an exacting idea-driven philosophy that pushes beyond what's already been done, Motion Theory's veteran directors have created award-winning campaigns for Hewlett-Packard, Nike, Budweiser, EA Sports, Toyota, and many other major companies, as well as notable music videos for such artists as Beck, REM, David Gray, and Papa Roach. In addition, the company's unique directing, design, and visual-effects work has been widely recognized by the AICP, the Art Directors Club, the MVPA, D&AD, and the Clio Festival.

STEPS TO CREATION

In *It Consolidates*, the complications of everyday life are simplified rather whimsically by the power of Hewlett-Packard's newest enterprise server.

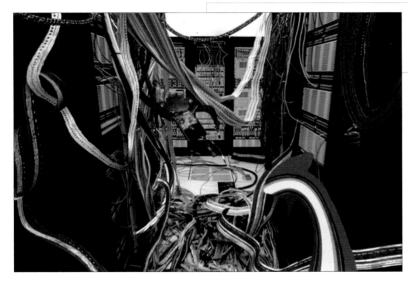  

Motion Theory integrated live-action and animation techniques to meld art and film, creating a unique style that illustrates the message in myriad everyday situations. Over the course of the spot, a tangle of freeways becomes a unified highway; a messy cubicle cleans itself; and a chaotic office folds into its most organized form. The runaway consolidation ends in the server room, where the HP enterprise server tames an unruly tangle of server wires.

The process began with the studio's design team working with illustrators to create the basis of a hyper-real cityscape. This illustrated vision was then laid over a series of motion-control and traditional camera shots, bringing a painterly, vibrant appearance to images of freeways, cities, and office cubicles. The artists and designers then worked in Maya and After Effects to merge CG techniques, stop-motion animation, and in-camera effects to convey the themes of artful consolidation.

TOOLS
Adobe After Effects, Adobe Illustrator, Adobe Photoshop, Apple Final Cut Pro, Autodesk Maya

CREDITS
Directors: John Norman, Rick Condos, Hunter Hindman
Art Director: Stacy Milrany
Producers: Elizabeth O'Toole, Hilary Bradley, Javier Jimenez, Scott Gemmell
Artists: Joseph Hart, Carm Goode, Daniel Chang, Ryan Wallace
Editors: Jeff Consiglio, Brad Watanabe

MOTION THEORY
TITLE: WRAPSHEAR
CLIENT: REEBOK INTERNATIONAL
FORMAT: TV COMMERCIAL

STEPS TO CREATION

An entire city bursts out of a shoe, presenting an increasingly difficult series of obstacles for an agile runner equipped with a new pair of Reebok Wrapshear shoes.

Motion Theory's directors and designers combined forces in order to create the burgeoning city, which seamlessly integrates LA locations and computer-generated architecture. As the city evolves, it presents the runner with an escalating series of challenges, including rising construction barriers, shifting walls, and falling objects. A primal, percussion-driven music track sets a vigorous pace along the way, leading to a finale in which the runner effortlessly springs over the final obstacle and sends the city retreating back into the shoe.

To achieve the look, live action was combined with CG to build a composite city, blurring the line between what is real and what is not. Careful planning was needed to achieve the transitions. Before filming, an extensive CG previsualization was created. The plan was to capture the stunts and complex maneuvers in the studio, and the simpler running footage out in the city. Nearly every shot in the spot combines real and CG elements.

TOOLS
Adobe After Effects, Adobe Illustrator, Adobe Photoshop, Apple Final Cut Pro, Apple Shake, Autodesk Maya

CREDITS
Directors: Warren Eakins, Randy Van Kleeck
Art Directors: Warren Eakins, Jesse Raker, Mark Kudsi
Producer: Katya Bankowsky

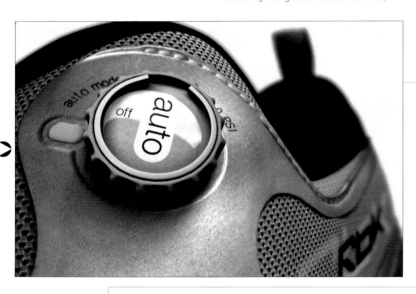

THE MOVING PICTURE COMPANY
UK
TITLE: CHANNEL 4
CLIENT: CHANNEL 4
FORMAT: NETWORK IDs

PROFILE

The Moving Picture Company (MPC) is a British postproduction facility that creates high-end digital visual effects and computer animation for international television, feature films, advertising, and the music industry.

MPC has dedicated character-animation and R&D teams that produce the software programs required to make the effects wholly believable. MPC has created animation and special effects for such high-profile projects as Terry Pratchett's *Hogfather*, BBC's *Bleak House*, Brett Ratner's *X-Men: The Last Stand*, Tim Burton's *Charlie and the Chocolate Factory* and *The Corpse Bride*, Ridley Scott's *Kingdom of Heaven*, and all Warner Bros *Harry Potter* films to date. Other projects include Roland Emmerich's *10,000 B.C.* and Andrew Adamson's *Narnia* saga.

STEPS TO CREATION

MPC was called on by UK-based Channel 4 to reinvent the network's original 1980s computer-animated logo. The new design combined naturalistic settings and advanced effects technology to show the various components of the figure "4" materializing from elements as diverse as bales of hay, power pylons, and motel signs.

Director Brett Foraker and effects supervisor Russell Appleford filmed various background plates of central London on a Mini DV camcorder, often hanging out of car windows to get the right perspective. Once these were approved, further background plates

were shot on Super 16 film. The camera angle was set perpendicular to the side of the car to give a view of side streets and alleyways slipping past. This provided a backdrop from which the logo would emerge. These shots were then graded in telecine and composited with Inferno.

To shoot the live-action foregrounds where the "4"s would ultimately sit, MPC used Super 35 film to ensure that there was as little grain as possible. This made later camera tracking in postproduction much easier. A three-month production stint ensued as Appleford and three other animators raced to produce the first series of idents.

The 3D animation was done using Maya, and involved Appleford and his team creating wire-frame models of each block that made up the figure "4." The blocks were rendered and the relevant textures applied to ensure that they appeared to be part of the environment. The animated elements were then tracked into the backgrounds.

Once all these elements were available, the compositing stage began. The lead operator, Mark Stannard, painstakingly matched the 3D "block" elements to the live-action foreground and background plates. Once the rigged "4"s were sitting correctly in the shots, 3D lighting and textures had to be corrected to ensure that they were perfectly integrated throughout.

TOOLS
2d3 Boujou, Autodesk Inferno, Autodesk Maya

CREDITS
Director: Brett Foraker
Producers: Jo Dillon, Gwilym Gwillim
3D Visual Effects Supervisor: Russell Appleford
Lead Compositing: Mark Stannard

NAILGUN*
USA
TITLE: MAN OF ACTION
CLIENT: SPIKE TV
FORMAT: NETWORK ID

PROFILE

With a strong belief that great art derives from making creative choices and sticking to them, veteran graphic designer Michael Waldron and editor/animator Erik van der Wilden launched Nailgun* in 2003. Since its inception, the BDA Gold Award-winning creative shop has been pushing the boundaries and exceeding client demands in its work for top advertising agencies and broadcast networks. Clients include ABC News, HBO, HGTV, Publicis, and McCann-Erickson.

STEPS TO CREATION

Spike TV had a new and improved branding slogan, "Get More Action," and wanted Nailgun* to create an image spot. It had to be adaptable—meaning it should be easy to update—and had to feature real-life and fictional "men of action." The men ranged from Benjamin Franklin and Wilt Chamberlain to Vic Mackey of the TV drama *The Shield*. Spike TV left the creative brief wide open, the only restriction being that the spot had to be a template for future installments that would have different characters.

At its initial brainstorming session, the Nailgun* team came up with all kinds of iconic imagery to represent "men of action." To keep the spot adaptable, it was important that most of the imagery was generic enough to work with any man of action. As future installments were intended to feature different characters, a quick refreshing of a couple of icons would work as a whole new spot.

For Benjamin Franklin, pods were developed to house both his image and the icons. The camera then flew from scene to scene to connect all the pods.

Hand-drawn images were blended with icons and photos. Scanned textures were also incorporated and made the spot look a bit roughed up around the edges. The "electricity" was built around the archival image of Franklin flying a kite. It was made in After Effects and mixed with the hand-drawn clouds. The silhouettes were shot in the studio with a DV camera over a makeshift green screen. The explosions from the tanks were made with a particle generator. The rest of the spot was a mixture of After Effects, Cinema 4D, Photoshop, and Illustrator.

TOOLS
Adobe After Effects, Adobe Illustrator, Adobe Photoshop, Autodesk Maya, Maxon Cinema 4D, pencil and paper

CREDITS
Creative Director: Michael Waldron
Director of Animation/Editor: Erik van der Wilden
Managing Producer: Elena Olivares
Design/Postproduction: Nailgun*
Design/Animation: Dae Hyuk Park
Animation: Jong Soo Kim
3D Animation: Roger Hom

NAILGUN*

TITLE: UNTAMED TV
CLIENT: INDEMAND NETWORKS
FORMAT: NETWORK ID

STEPS TO CREATION

Indemand Networks approached Nailgun* with Untamed TV, a new programming block in need of branding. The new channel planned to air everything from uncensored comedy shows to the infamous *Girls Gone Wild* franchise, and needed a clever way to promote this unusual mix.

Nailgun* came up with the idea of having the viewer fly through an environment made up of censorship tape, finally breaking through into the world of Untamed TV. Through the journey, the viewer would discover a variety of metaphors for the network content, with the images resolving to reveal the flaming Untamed TV logo.

The beginning of the spot is a blend of Illustrator artwork and an illustration of two ears made to move like a butterfly. These are animated using the After Effects 3D camera.

The Untamed TV environment was built as a large Photoshop file that was imported into After Effects. Each individual element was animated separately and then placed into an animated 3D camera move. The potpourri explosions from the guns were created using a particle generator in After Effects. The background was a huge vertical file created in Photoshop that could be moved vertically without the risk of running out of real estate.

The 3D egg that pops out of the landscape was created in Autodesk Maya, then rendered out and placed back into After Effects. The cracking and explosion that leads to the birth of the television in the logo was also created in Maya. The flames that burst from the television are individual Photoshop layers that were cut together to give the effect of burning.

TOOLS
Adobe After Effects, Adobe Illustrator, Adobe Photoshop, Autodesk Maya

CREDITS
Creative Director: Michael Waldron
Director of Animation: Erik van der Wilden
Producer: Elena Olivares
Lead Design/2D Animation: Dae Hyuk Park
3D Animation: Santiago Castaño

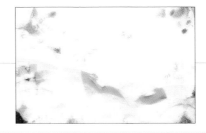

ODEON
POLAND
TITLE: CHICKENS
CLIENT: ODEON RYBARCZYK PRODUCTIONS
FORMAT: PROMOTIONAL E-CARD

PROFILE

Leszek Rybarczyk, Odeon's founder, studied architecture at Warsaw Polytechnic; he caught the director's bug when he went on to study scenography at the Academy of Fine Arts in Warsaw. At first, he worked under famous Polish directors, but in the late 1980s Rybarczyk became inspired by the developing movie industry in the United States, and decided to set up his own company.

Since that time, Rybarczyk has produced and directed hundreds of commercials, making Odeon the leader in spot production in Poland. Odeon specializes in commercial production and postproduction, providing complete services with technical facilities for all creative needs. One of Odeon's powerful assets is its animation department, in which traditional hand-drawn, Flash, 3D, CGI, and stop-motion animation are all produced. The Odeon team of directors, animators, modelers, and illustrators creates special effects for commercials, music videos, and films.

STEPS TO CREATION

Chickens is actually an Easter e-card. It was used as a promotion and a celebration of Odeon's fifteenth anniversary, and served as a showcase for the studio's talents and various facilities. The rooster symbolizes Odeon's founder, Rybarczyk, while the pink hen, furiously knitting the colorful scarf, symbolizes efficiency and creativity. Quality casting is represented by the chicken in a bikini, and high-end special effects are represented by the futuristic robot chicken called the Henminator. A clutch of "production" eggs goes through a "postproduction" machine, which turns them into decorated Easter eggs.

The creators wanted a look that was photo-realistic yet highly stylized. They also wanted the look of a stop-motion film. Aardman's *Chicken Run* and the penguin from Nick Park's *The Wrong Trousers* were big influences.

LightWave 3D was used to model the objects, while the animation and rendering were done in Maya. The

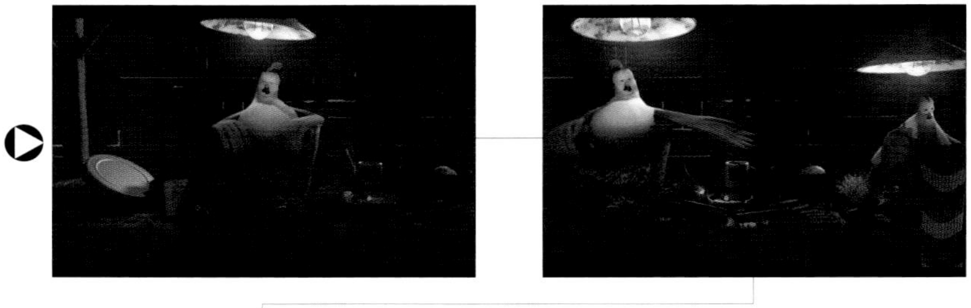

problem of creating realistic straw in the henhouse was solved by Maya's paint effect.

Modeling started after the layout and character design had been approved. Dummy objects were then made, so work could start on a 3D animatic. Animation was based on the time and spacing given by the director. As the set slowly began to take shape, lights and textures were added to the scene. The rendered frames were divided into three main layers: the henhouse, the chickens, and the Easter egg machine. Rendering

was relatively quick: one frame in 720p HD-resolution took about four minutes on a Dual Xeon 2.8 Mhz computer using Maya. Such results were possible because there were no ray-traced lights and surfaces used, except for the Henminator, which had a highly reflective coat. The creation of the Easter egg machine also took a good deal of time. Various pieces of concept art and several 3D models were made before the final version was settled on. The final compositing was done in Autodesk Smoke. The cutout animation of Warsaw, the Polish capital, which is

visible in the henhouse window, was added as a reference to Odeon's location.

TOOLS
Autodesk Maya, Autodesk Smoke, NewTek LightWave 3D

CREDITS
Director: Nicolas Valencia
Animation: Alan Shamsudin, Rafa Bielski, Piotr Wysocki
Modeling: Paweł Tybora, Paweł Krawczyk, Rafa Bielski, Mateusz Subieta, Piotr Wysocki
Rendering: Rafa Bielski, Piotr Wysocki

ODEON
TITLE: THE BEAR
CLIENT: ODEON RYBARCZYK PRODUCTIONS
FORMAT: SHORT FILM

STEPS TO CREATION

An advertising agency, wanting a sample of Odeon's work, asked the company to create, in a CG environment, an animation of a humanoid bear with a look similar to that of Shrek. Since this was basically a screen test, the animators thought it would be funny if the bear were screen-tested on a set.

The bear was given a contradictory character: cute and cuddly on the outside, but a slob within. He smokes and reads erotic magazines whenever he can, and even sneaks a beer backstage.

With the initial idea drafted, Odeon decided to present the backdrop just as it would appear in a film or commercial. Canvas-painted landscape and polystyrene foam trees were created to emphasize the irony of the situation. There was also the ever-popular blue screen, which is often seen in the editing room before any effects are applied to a film.

The result was pleasing to both the studio and the agency, but the project never came to fruition and the commercial was canceled. However, the film has lived on as a promotion for

Odeon, and is quite popular at animation festivals.

The first step was to create the bear. A good number of drawings and sketches were produced before there was a design of which everyone approved. The bear was drawn and imported into LightWave 3D for the modeler to use as a reference. UV textures were hand-drawn in Photoshop using a Wacom tablet to create the colors needed for Sasquatch, a hair and fur plug-in. Lukasz Pazera's Auto Character Setup made the rigging process a breeze. When that was done,

one animator continued working with the bear while the rest of the team worked on the set. A rough layout was drawn and later modeled. Sasquatch was used again to create the grass.

The film was rendered in High Definition (1280 x 720) at 25 fps. Using the RPF file format with its useful object ID, Z-buffer, and numerous extra channels made it easy to mask trees, add fog, fix textures, and perform color correction. All that was possible without having to render each element in a separate pass. The scene was divided into seven layers: bear's fur, the bear,

foreground log, ground, grass, trees, and the background image of the plain. All this was later put together in Fusion, where such atmospheric effects as light shafts and floating dust particles were added.

TOOLS
Adobe Photoshop, Eyeon Fusion, Lukasz Pazera Auto Character Setup, NewTek LightWave 3D, Wacom tablet, Worley Laboratories Sasquatch

CREDITS
Director: Mikołaj Valencia
Animation/Design: Alan Shamsudin
Modeling: Paweł Tybora, Paweł Krawczyk

PANOPTIC
USA
TITLE: PLANET X
CLIENT: SCION
FORMAT: WEB CARTOON

PROFILE

PanOptic is both an artists' collective and a video production company, and is dedicated to directing and designing material for television, film, video installations, and interfaces. The collective/company postulates that the proliferation of technologies has allowed for a restructuring of our perceptions of space. From video games, in which people navigate through a constructed environment, to onboard car mapping used to drive through the real world, there is an increasing reliance on digitally created vision. By adopting the languages and visual methodology of technology, PanOptic has created means of navigating these real and imaginary places.

STEPS TO CREATION

The Scion car company asked PanOptic to do a short viral marketing piece with the brief: "do whatever you want." The team were inspired by Alejandro Jodorowsky's film *The Holy Mountain* to invent a company world on the newly

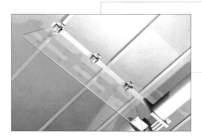

discovered tenth planet, Xena—the Planet X of the cartoon's title. The company runs a commercial art factory, staffed by a race of blue-skinned, chain-smoking, gossiping slackers. The story in part revolves around the nonsensical sexual relations between the characters. The world on Planet X is chaotic and mystical, and for the most part does away with the laws of physics.

The process began with an animatic drawn straight into a Wacom Cintiq and edited in After Effects. The final timing was figured out at this stage. Once the timing was locked,

the animation director began work on the key frames and breakdowns for the character animation. This stage was done in much the same way as old-school cel animation, except that it was entirely digital. Once the key frames were set, the CG artist began locking up the angles of the background and the details in the modeling. As the sets were being built, the inbetweeners went through the process of digitally hand-drawing the remaining frames, handing them off to be colored. After the character animation had been finished, the frames went into

compositing, where the CG elements were mixed with hand-drawn elements to form a cohesive world.

The penultimate stage was done in After Effects. All the scenes were assembled and such special effects as lights, explosions, and finishing touches were added. The final stage was sound design, which was done in-house on Pro Tools. This all-digital process allowed PanOptic both the flexibility to adjust the animation in real time and the ability to monitor constantly the process in the digital realm.

TOOLS
Adobe After Effects, Digidesign Pro Tools, Wacom Cintiq

CREDITS
Direction: PanOptic
Creative Director: Gary Breslin
Producer: Javier Hernandez
2D Animation/Story: Daniel Cardenas
3D Animation: Nick Fischer
Sound Design: Daniel Perlin

JANET PERLMAN
CANADA
TITLE: BULLY DANCE
CLIENT: NATIONAL FILM BOARD OF CANADA
FORMAT: SHORT FILM

PROFILE

Janet Perlman is a writer and director of humorous short films. Her work has received international acclaim, including an Academy Award nomination, an Emmy, and many festival grand prizes. Her extensive work with the National Film Board of Canada includes *The Tender Tale of Cinderella Penguin*, *Why Me?*, *Dinner for Two*, and *Bully Dance*.

Perlman also writes and illustrates children's books, and she has taught animation at Harvard University and at the Rhode Island School of Design. Her latest book, *The Delicious Bug*, will be published in 2008.

STEPS TO CREATION

Bully Dance is the story of a dance class in which a bully repeatedly teases and intimidates a smaller member of the group. Eventually, the victim and the community are forced to deal with the bully, who is himself a victim in his own home.

Perlman's films are humorous and sometimes downright silly, but there is

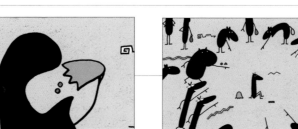
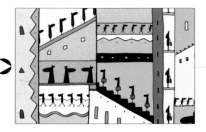

usually an underlying important message in them. She puts much time and effort into the story, and never starts animating until she feels that everything works.

Perlman generally develops the characters and design to fit a particular idea or subject matter. In this case, she wanted *Bully Dance* to be a universal story that could happen anywhere—thus, there are no human characters, and the setting is unspecific.

At the writing/storyboard stage, Perlman developed the visuals and the story in parallel. She drew up the storyboard and scanned the drawings into the computer to make an animatic. There were no words to write, as the story was to be told solely through dance and music; the action and characterization were to be conveyed through gesture and body language. Before the animation began, composer Judith Gruber-Stitzer created a guide track to which all the movement was timed, thus inspiring the characters' dance moves.

Perlman tested the animation at every phase and compiled all the scenes as they were completed, in order that she could see how sequences worked and fitted together.

All the animation was drawn on paper, using felt-tip pens for their heavy line quality. The drawings were scanned into the computer, where they were composited and colored, and the camera moves were added. Dust and debris were added manually to the backgrounds to avoid that flat and clean computer look.

TOOLS
Adobe Photoshop, Adobe Premiere, Corel Painter, felt-tip pens and paper, Softimage Toonz

CREDITS
Director/Animation: Janet Perlman
Producers: Marcy Page, David Verrall
Animation Assistance: Luigi Allemano, Sylvain Lavoie
Music Composition: Judith Gruber-Stitzer

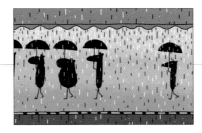

FONS SCHIEDON
THE NETHERLANDS
TITLE: HAPPY VIOLENT BUGS
CLIENT: MTV ASIA
FORMAT: NETWORK IDs

PROFILE

Fons Schiedon is a writer, director, and illustrator who has worked for such diverse entities and projects as *Esquire* magazine, Peter Greenaway's online game *Tulse Luper Journey*, motion graphics for the 2004 documentary *Sneakers*, music videos, commercials, and animated shorts, as well as network IDs for Nickelodeon and MTV Asia. He also writes and directs *Mobbed* and *Mob Squad* (see page 146), a biweekly animated series for MTV Asia.

STEPS TO CREATION

While this series of five MTV IDs was made for TV broadcast, they were mainly constructed for use on mobile phones. Since phone screens are so small and video quality is generally low, the images had to be exceptionally sharp. That set the tone for the design.

It was decided that the IDs would cover life as we know it, in under two minutes. Violently happy bugs live, die, fight, procreate, and eat food from a burger joint, all located inside a phone. The bugs' appearances had to be

stylized and minimal. If a bug didn't need arms, it wouldn't get them. Faces rather than body language are the expressive tool.

An outline for five short films was written and approved by the client. Eighteen characters were chosen from a pool of thirty. The shorts were animated in Flash, without the use of a storyboard or animatic. Animated scenes were exported into the Premiere-editing timeline to see how they related to other scenes, and also to find out what else was needed.

Halfway through the process, a version was sent to the sound designer,

who worked on a rhythmic score. This same mute version was also sent to MTV for approval.

The scores from the audio sessions were added to the timeline, and minor adjustments made to the animation or editing as necessary. When all the scenes were done, the Flash animation was imported into After Effects, where additional camera movements were added and color correction geared for TV broadcast. This version was sent to the sound designer for a final mix. The five clips took three weeks to produce.

TOOLS
Adobe After Effects, Adobe Illustrator, Adobe Premiere Pro, Macromedia Flash

CREDITS
Director/Design/Animation: Fons Schiedon
Director at MTV Asia: Charmaine Choo
Music/Sound Design: Bram Meindersma

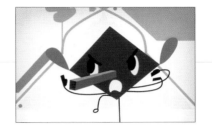

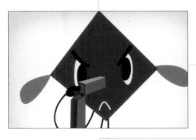

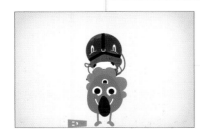

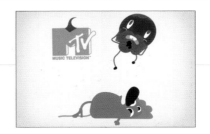

FONS SCHIEDON
TITLE: MOBBED/MOB SQUAD
CLIENT: MTV ASIA/MOTOROLA
FORMAT: SHORT FEATURES

STEPS TO CREATION

Mobbed was created as a multiplatform concept by MTV Asia. Episode lengths ranged from thirty to eighty seconds; they were output on MTV, on a website that functioned as a Motorola user platform, and as downloadable content for mobile phones and toys. The three main characters of *Mobbed* are Gus, Lenny, and Donny Sunshine, who also star in their own biweekly miniseries, *Mob Squad*.

Production of each *Mob Squad* episode took two weeks and was

worked on simultaneously in Amsterdam, São Paulo in Brazil, and Singapore. Each started with a written treatment, which consisted of about ten lines describing events. After the outline was approved by MTV, an animatic was made. The animatic, with models for characters and prop designs, was sent to the animation studio, where all the materials were checked. The animation studio would regularly send scenes and "digital pencil tests" via MSN Messenger, so suggestions or alternative approaches would find their way into the episodes.

Animators worked with a rough version first. Once approved, the animation would go to be colorized, cleaned up, and uploaded to a server. The animation was done in Flash and exported as image sequences for processing in After Effects. There, the character animation was combined with 2D or 3D backgrounds. Camera movements and effects were also added to the scenes. Meanwhile, the early rough version was sent to the sound designer, who started work on the sound effects and a score. As his proposals came in, they were reviewed

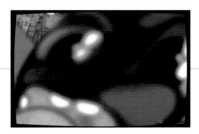

directly in the editing environment so that any timing issues could be resolved. The compositing and soundtrack were finalized together.

A final edit was made, color correction applied, and the soundtrack mixed for broadcast. When the episode was approved at MTV, a hi-res version was uploaded for broadcast.

TOOLS
Adobe After Effects, Adobe Illustrator, Adobe Premiere Pro, Macromedia Flash, MSN Web Messenger

CREDITS
Director/Design/Writer: Fons Schiedon
Director at MTV Asia: Charmaine Choo
Live-action Producer: Janneke van de Kerkhof
Animation: Luciana Eguti, Paulo Muppet, Paula Indalencio
Music/Sound Design: Bram Meindersma

FONS SCHIEDON
TITLE: SUBMARINE CHANNEL LOGO TAG
CLIENT: SUBMARINE CHANNEL
FORMAT: NETWORK ID

STEPS TO CREATION

The Submarine Channel asked for a fifteen-second logo animation for its theatrical screenings and DVD releases. The brief was: "Something that suits us in the same way the horse suits Tristar."

Schiedon responded with a one-line treatment to describe his approach, plus a rough storyboard and a list of fifty possible objects. Submarine made a shortlist of its favorite objects. To see how many would fit into the fifteen seconds, tests were run using sketches and photographs.

The dolphin, squirrel, submarine, robot, couch, and Chinese takeout carton were modeled in 3D, using Blender. They were textured and rigged, and animated individually. The animations were imported directly in After Effects to check their position in the timeline. The water surface was animated separately and rendered, as was the backdrop, which was first painted in Photoshop and then imported into Blender. In After Effects, the different elements were all combined and the transitions between the objects were made using basic masking and morphing techniques.

 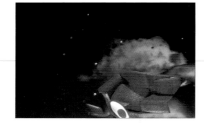  

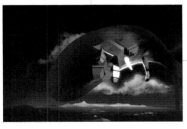

The first rough version was sent to the client for intermediate approval, and also to the sound designer so he could start work on the score.

Meanwhile, an HD-version of the trailer was rendered in Blender and imported into After Effects for fine tuning, addition of some final effects, and last-minute color correction.

The finished logo worked like an electric storm of associations, and gave an impression of the rich and unlimited world of possibilities that Submarine creates in its productions.

TOOLS
Adobe After Effects, Adobe Illustrator, Adobe Photoshop, Blender

CREDITS
Director/Design/Animation: Fons Schiedon
Sound Design: Tim Baker

J.J. SEDELMAIER PRODUCTIONS
USA
TITLE: LOOK WHAT YOU'VE DONE
CLIENT: MTV
FORMAT: NETWORK ID

PROFILE

J.J. Sedelmaier Productions was established in White Plains, New York, in 1990. The company produces animation, print, and corporate branding, and also serves as a reference resource for various historical research projects. It has produced cutting-edge animated TV commercials for such clients as Volkswagen, Slim Jim, and Hotwire; in entertainment, it was responsible for launching MTV's *Beavis and Butt-Head*, the hilarious cartoons on NBC's *Saturday Night Live*, and for developing the pilot episode of *Harvey Birdman, Attorney at Law* for Cartoon Network and the Tek Jansen cartoons for Comedy Central's *The Colbert Report*. It also provides illustration and design work for *Playboy*, *Esquire*, *Rolling Stone*, *Texas Monthly*, and the *Chicago Tribune*.

The studio has won hundreds of international film and design awards.

STEPS TO CREATION

According to Sedelmaier, creating a new ID for MTV's already well-known series of network IDs was really just an excuse to work with his friend, creator/designer/ artist Craig Yoe.

Yoe thought that a guy coming to the front door to pick up his date was a good premise. The guy rings the doorbell, which triggers his metamorphosis into a series of weird creatures that finally resolve into an MTV logo.

Sedelmaier called on Tony Eastman to animate the cartoon because, though Eastman can animate in a variety of styles, he naturally gravitates towards a cartoon sensibility.

Eastman and Sedelmaier's studio of animation artists went to work on creating the cartoon. First they did a sequential series of sketches (the

storyboard) that helped the production gel as a visual story.

Next, after compiling all of the designed drawings from Yoe, Eastman and Sedelmaier discussed how long the individual characters were going to appear on screen before transforming into the next creature. Eastman then translated the storyboard into animation by doing rough drawings and making the characters act their parts.

From here, the animation drawings were given to assistant animators, who added any additional drawings requested by Eastman and Sedelmaier. All these drawings were then exposed and viewed as a "pencil test"—a film of the rough animation that still allows for changes before the drawings are cleaned up in preparation for final coloring and checking.

Once Yoe, Eastman, and Sedelmaier were satisfied with the test, it went into final production. This entailed photocopying the images on to acetate, turning them over and painting colored acrylic vinyl on the reverse, and shooting all the artwork on 35-mm motion-picture film.

Musician/composer/sound designer Tom Pomposello added his expert touch with a killer soundtrack, which was recorded to the final color footage.

TOOLS
35-mm KEM flatbed editor, acetate celluloid (cels), animation bond paper, Cel-Vinyl acrylic paint, Graphic 3000 pens

CREDITS
Director/Producer/Editor: J.J. Sedelmaier
Production Coordinator: Irene Cerdas
Concept/Design/Artist: Craig Yoe
Animation: Tony Eastman
Animation Assistants: Tom Warburton, Bryon Moore
Sound Design: Tom Pomposello
Postproduction: Tape House Editorial

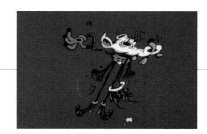

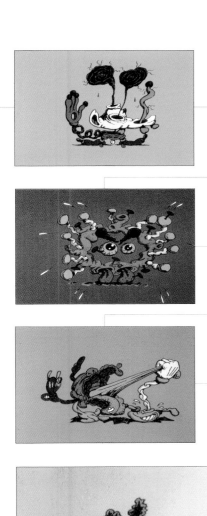

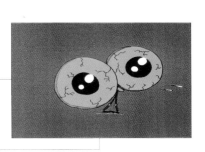

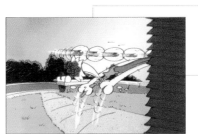

Ⅱ

SHILO
USA
TITLE: IMAGINE THIS
CLIENT: FUEL TV
FORMAT: NETWORK ID

PROFILE

Shilo is a collective of directors, designers, and animators who share a passion for forging new storytelling perspectives through design and visual effects. Shilo strives not only to push the boundaries of contemporary motion graphics and direction but also to galvanize an increasingly shock-proof audience. The studio endeavors to create projects with high emotional impact by combining live action, 3D CGI, classic typography, and illustration with music and sound design. It constantly reinvents its methodology to meet the needs of its growing client base. Shilo has studios in New York and San Diego.

STEPS TO CREATION

What would a skate park look like if it had been designed by M.C. Escher or Salvador Dali? A strange question to be sure, but it's the one that Shilo's creative team posed to Fuel TV after it had been asked to create a mind-blowing ID for the action-sports channel. The first step in the process

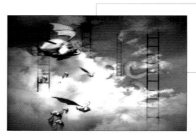

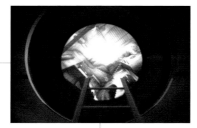

was the creation of an elaborate set of storyboards and 3D previsualizations of a skate park that took its design cues from Escher's fantastically impossible structures. The park was populated with Dalí-influenced characters: a gentleman who upon lifting his hat uncovers a hinged head with a ladder within it; a winged fish flying around; and two rabbit-headed human characters racing up and down ladders. The next stage

was to film skateboarders Danny Montoya and Brian Brown in action in a green-screen environment. This called for constantly referencing the previsualized "Escher world" to ensure that the camera angles, lighting, and focal lengths were correct for each scene, bearing in mind that in the final piece the skaters would be shown in impossible situations. For example, one skater would be in the foreground, while

a second would be skating upside down in the background, and a third would be skating up a wall elsewhere in the frame. Once the live-action elements were captured and digitized, the skateboarders were keyed so they could be removed from the green-screen backdrop they had been filmed against, and combined with the animated scenes that had been created simultaneously. After the finishing

touches had been placed on the visuals, the audio track was added by music- and sound-design 'shop' Polar Empire.

TOOLS
Adobe Illustrator, Adobe Photoshop, Apple Final Cut Pro, Autodesk Maya

CREDITS
Design/Production: Shilo (New York/San Diego)
Music/Sound Design: Polar Empire

SHILO
TITLE: SCION xA SHADOW
CLIENT: TOYOTA MOTOR SALES USA/SCION
FORMAT: TV + FILM COMMERCIAL

STEPS TO CREATION

The challenge was to create a spot promoting Toyota's sports car, the Scion xA Shadow, for both cinematic release and traditional broadcast.

The process began with the design of mood boards and preparation of a written treatment. From there a full set of hand-drawn storyboards was created. These detailed key shots, camera moves, transitions, and the overall flow of the spot. Owing to the complexity of the animation, a good deal of time was invested in previsualizing

the spot in the CG environment. A rough animation of the entire sequence was crafted with Maya, which helped determine what worked and what didn't, as well as to work out texture resolutions, camera angles, and so on.

While previsualizations and the animatic were being worked on, modelers were busy developing an entire virtual set for the dark and mysterious digital city the car would ride through. Artists created hundreds of layered images, such as various brick patterns, cement, grime, and signage, which would blanket the 3D geometry.

The look was to be realistic but with a highly stylized flavor that would reveal itself in new ways each time the spot was viewed.

As the production moved along, the animators were constantly generating multipass renders. These were then imported into After Effects, where they were composited together. It is labor-intensive to render multiple passes and break out each element, but it was imperative in order to be able to adjust such minute details as the light hitting an object, and the reflection from the car's windows, body paint, and chrome.

During this phase, other visual elements were being added to the various scenes, and the look was being continually refined. Smoke, fog, sparks, and various other effects were integrated into the appropriate scenes, enhancing the spot's hybridized photo-real look.

TOOLS
Adobe Illustrator, Adobe Photoshop, Apple Final Cut Pro, Autodesk Maya

CREDITS
Creative Directors: Andre Stringer, Jose Gomez
Executive Producer: Tracy Chandler
Animation: Marco Giampaolo, Eric Bauer, Henning Koczy, Marc Boutges
3D Modeling: Cody Smith, Scott Denton
CG Artists: Philip Benn, Kirk Cadrette, Long-Hai Pham, Oliver Arnold, Ryan Lorie, Russell Pearsall, Yoshiya Yamada
Flame Compositing: Jennifer German, MB Emigh
Matte Painting: Allen Battino, Dark Hoffma

ALEXANDRE SIQUEIRA
PORTUGAL
TITLE: BELINVICTA
CLIENT: ICAM
FORMAT: SHORT FILM

PROFILE

Alexandre Siqueira's obsession with the illusion of movement began when he was six years old. He was browsing through a science book on his father's desk when he noticed a sequence of photograms depicting a boxing fight that had been used to illustrate the amazing world of animation.

After finishing an image and communication course at the Soares dos Reis Art School in Oporto, Portugal, Siqueira codirected *Sopa fria* (Cold Soup), which was produced in the puppet animation course at CITEN, Lisbon. In 2000, he returned to Oporto and collaborated in several projects at Filmografo Studio. Between 2004 and 2005, he started teaching animation at the Oficinas da Imagem in Maia, where he produced the short film *Vôos pela imaginação* (Flights Through Imagination), directed by his teenage students.

Siqueira has also directed *Fábulas urbanas* (Urban Fables).

STEPS TO CREATION

To create a film, Siqueira always starts with an idea and a message that he wants to share with the viewer. *Belinvicta* is about a lonely boy who falls in love, and his subsequent tragic adventure in Oporto, the Portuguese city on the River Douro. The film's title is a fusion of the Portuguese words *bela*, "beauty," and *invicta*, "glorious," an adjective that in Portugal is mostly used to to identify the city of Oporto.

Once the idea was realized, with the help of a screenwriter, Siqueira developed the synopsis, script, and dialogue. In the meantime, he sketched the main characters, the backgrounds, and the storyboards. This planning phase is the part of the process that Siqueira likes best. He loves the solitude of working on his own, when he feels he can "travel" into the drawings and interact with the characters.

Siqueira put together a team, and together they created layouts of the scenes, using Maya to get a sense of the proportions of the physical space. From there they created the blocking, which is like an animatic but in 3D.

Finally, they developed the models in the finest detail, paying particular attention to hair, fur, cloth, and so on, to convey a realistic appearance.

TOOLS
Adobe Photoshop, Adobe Premiere, Autodesk Combustion, Autodesk Maya

CREDITS
Director: Alexandre Siqueira
Producers: Appia Filmes, Luis Pedro Martins, Pedro Gonçalves
Writer: Jorge Palinhos
Animation: Ricardo Silva, Sandra Murta, Marco Godinho, Pedro Pinho
Music Composition: Dead Combo

STUDIO AKA
UK
TITLE: THE BIG WIN
CLIENT: CAMELOT
FORMAT: TV COMMERCIAL

PROFILE

Studio aka is a London-based animation studio that has won countless awards for its work from D&AD and the British Academy of Film and Television Arts (BAFTA), among others.

STEPS TO CREATION

The Big Win was commissioned for the UK National Lottery. The brief from the ad agency, AMV BBDO, was simple: a man is given a bag of smiles and hands them out to everyone he meets. The ad takes its stylistic inspiration from such material as the Dr. Seuss stories and other children's books, including *The Moomins* and *Where the Wild Things Are*; director Marc Craste mixed in references to European folktale animation style and created Milo, the central character.

The first hurdle was getting the client to approve Milo, so short test sequences were created; one showed Milo driving his idiosyncratic car through a fog-bound street, another showed him walking jauntily along. The client was

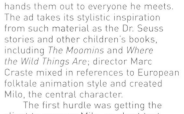

convinced and gave the green light to start the rest of the project design, development, and building.

Overall, initial pencil sketches were translated into 3D by aka's animation department. Images were then built and animated in Softimage XSI; compositing was done in After Effects.

Scenes were created from an initial pencil animatic (camera moves applied to a storyboard) and an approved blockomatic (a crude "block through," in which non-animated characters are positioned and placed for each scene). Models were then rigged and built

according to each scene. The animators created the performance for each of the characters based on the director's boards, animatic, and scene briefing. Once these were approved, they were sent along the pipeline to be textured, lit, and rendered.

Each scene is made up of multiple layers of animation, set backgrounds, and lighting and effect passes. When these layers are composited, it allows for grading and adjustments to be made. Initially the spot was to have been lip-synched by a full cast, but following a mid-stage process meeting,

it was felt that the spot would adhere more closely to the original "smile" concept if the voice stayed off screen.

A potential problem was that too many scenes had been scripted for the running time, but this was partly solved by using a split screen, which allowed four scenes to be played simultaneously. This solution had the further advantage of also working well stylistically.

TOOLS
Adobe After Effects, Adobe Photoshop, pencil and paper, Softimage XSI

CREDITS
Director: Marc Craste
Production: Studio aka

ARTHUR SUYDAM
USA
TITLE: ADVENTURES OF CHOLLY AND FLYTRAP
CLIENT: PARANOID DELUSIONS
FORMAT: SHORT FILM

PROFILE

Arthur Suydam is a master draftsman and teller of haunting stories. He first came to prominence on the comic-art scene in the 1970s with his innovative marrying of classical painting and comic art. His work helped revolutionize the industry and began the comic renaissance of the 1980s. This, in turn, opened doors for mainstream writers and artists to create literature for a more mature readership. Suydam's signature work includes *The Original Adventures of Cholly and Flytrap*, *Mudwogs*, and art for the *Marvel Zombies* series.

Recently, Suydam was honored with the Spectrum Gold Medal for artistic excellence; an induction into the Society of Illustrators; and Lifetime Achievement awards from the University of Maryland and the San Sebastian Film Festival. Currently, he is working on several movie and animation projects.

STEPS TO CREATION

According to Eric Chu, animation partner at the Paranoid Delusions animation studio, "Making *Cholly and Flytrap* was a relatively easy process. I honestly didn't have much to do. It was all there on the page: Arthur had done it for me already."

Since the animation process itself can be described as boring, tedious, and time-consuming, before anything else, it is important to have the story right. The storyboard came first, and it was very tight: it is always easier to fix shots on paper than later in the editing room. The designs came next, and these let the characters' personalities find their own interesting shapes and gestures. The modeling was done after that. Softimage XSI was used for the basic characters, and the details were added with ZBrush and a Wacom tablet, which give the models a more organic, sculptural look.

To find the colors and textures that support the characters without overpowering them, the hue/saturation sliders in Photoshop were used to try out different colors. Softimage was used for UV-mapping and texturing.

The next step was the lighting. This can make or break a shot, since color and intensity go a long way toward setting the mood in the scene. Placement helps separate the characters from the background and directs the audience's attention to where the animators want it.

For the most part, animation was done by hand. Motion-capture software is useful for elements that need to integrate with live action, but it can tend to look a little creepy and distracting when used in a nonrealistic animated film. In the hands of a good animator, the models cease to be computer representations and become living, breathing characters, ready to wreak havoc on the world.

TOOLS
Adobe Photoshop, Pixologic ZBrush, SoftimageXSI, Wacom tablet

CREDITS
Director: Arthur Suydam
Lead Animation: Eric Chu

PROFILE

Tak Productions West is a full-service Los Angeles-based video and film production house, which is headed by Glenn Takakjian.

As a producer, director, writer, editor, and 3D animator, Takakjian has provided production and postproduction services, as well as motion graphics and 3D animation, for a number of TV shows, commercials, and infomercials. He is currently one of the lead animators for the History Channel's hit show *Modern Marvels*.

STEPS TO CREATION

Projects for the History Channel's *Modern Marvels* usually start with a request for a visualization of those things that cannot be photographed. Accordingly, Takakjian has created animations of such weather systems as hurricanes and storm surges, all sorts of machinery, buildings, landscapes, water, and even outer space. Generally, multiple custom models need to be built to illustrate the "inner workings" of things; for example, cross-sections of machines, the insides of the human

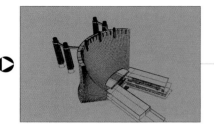

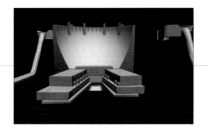
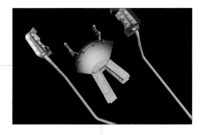

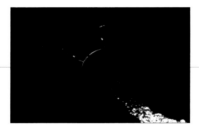

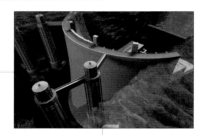

body, and the formation of a snowflake. It takes about three weeks to design and execute these two- to six-minute highly technical animations.

Takakjian starts with research to make sure he fully understands the process he's going to visualize. Then he designs an animation that is visually compelling yet simple enough for the audience to understand. Next, he builds accurate models and their surrounding environments, which are then texture-mapped and lit. As a filmmaker, he likes to give the animations a "cinematic" feel by incorporating dynamic and dramatic

camera moves: he feels that each animation should tell a little story.

Some of the animations require highly complex software. Takakjian generally uses Cinema 4D because of its stability, its amazingly fast render engine, and its powerful modeling tools.

The model of the Hoover Dam was constructed using primitives (basic geometric shapes), NURBS ("Non-Uniform Rational B-Splines," or mathematical representations of 3D geometry), and booleans (shapes created from two different shapes). Construction was based on various

photographs and "eyeballed." The initial model was texture-mapped using Cinema 4D's internal texture controls, and some textures were created in Photoshop.

TOOLS
Adobe After Effects, Adobe Photoshop, Allume Poser, Macromedia Freehand, Maxon Cinema 4D

CREDITS
Design/Animation: Glenn Takakjian
Modeling: John Starr Dewar, Glenn Takakjian

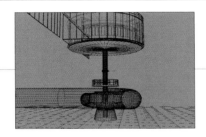
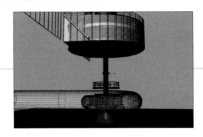
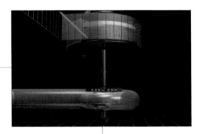

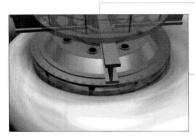
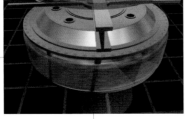
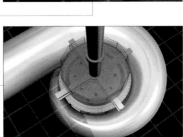

TANDEM FILMS
UK
TITLE: FLATWORLD
CLIENT: BBC TWO
FORMAT: TV FEATURE

PROFILE

Tandem Films is a London-based studio that was formed by directors Daniel Greaves and Nigel Pay to cater to advertising, broadcast, and independent animation productions.

Flatworld, a thirty-minute animation directed by Greaves for Tandem, has won more than thirty international awards, including seventeen for best film. Other highly acclaimed work by Greaves includes *Manipulation*, which won the Academy Award for best animated short in 1992, and *Little Things* (2004), which gathered twenty-six international awards. At the time of writing, Greaves has two projects in production: *Mixed Notes* and *Speechless*.

STEPS TO CREATION

The idea originated as a sketch of the world as a flat disk. The feature was to show how "Flatworld" was formed from sheets of paper floating in a cosmos cluttered with office ery. This world needed to look as if it had been constructed from paper, card, and

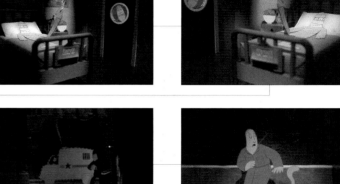

stationery items. The design was a collaboration between Greaves, set designer Gordon Allen, and lighting and camera operator Simon Paul.

Storyboards were drawn and each scene was animated using the traditional pencil-on-paper technique. Once this had been tested on video and approved, it was photocopied and colored by a team of artworkers, mounted on cards, cut out with scalpels, reinforced with lead weights, and numbered sequentially. Twelve characters were used for twenty-four frames. More than 40,000 cutout characters were

needed, each of which took more than an hour to complete.

Once the characters were finished, they were placed on a 3D set and filmed frame by frame. Various templates and marking systems were used to ensure exact positioning. Sets were constructed entirely from paper and card, and took approximately three months to create. They were lit in a rich, live-action style before being filmed. A core team of forty people worked on the film, although over a hundred were involved.

Animation went into full production in January 1996, and all shooting was

complete by December. The effects scenes were composited on various film-resolution computers at many facility houses in London's Soho district. All the sound effects were recorded or created by Russell Pay over a period of eight months. The score was composed by Julian Nott and recorded in Prague using a ninety-two-piece orchestra. Sound and music were synched to picture and mixed together during a week-long sound edit.

TOOLS
Autodesk Discreet Flame, Kodak Cineon, pencil and paper, Quantel Domino, Quantel Henry

CREDITS
Director: Daniel Greaves
Director of Photography: Simon Paul
Producer: Nigel Pay
Writers: Daniel Greaves, Patrick Veale
Set Design: Gordon Allen
Music: Julian Nott
Sound Effects: Russell Pay

VELVET MEDIENDESIGN
GERMANY
TITLE: ARION MUSIC AWARDS
CLIENT: MEGA CHANNEL, GREECE
FORMAT: EVENT DESIGN PACKAGE

PROFILE

Matthias Zentner and Andrea Bednarz founded Velvet Mediendesign in Munich, Germany, in order to further their shared passion for design and their constant search for varied creative stimuli.

Velvet describes itself as a group of individuals, each contributing his or her know-how and experience. In terms of work methodology, each project features different team members, variously making use of designers, concept makers, creative directors, animators, 3D specialists, operators, directors, producers, editors, copywriters, musicians, and software developers.

Velvet is divided into a design studio and a film-production company. Flexibility is essential to its philosophy to adapt to each client's specific requirements, target audiences, and strategic objectives.

STEPS TO CREATION

The Arion Music Awards are the annual Greek awards presented by the Mega Channel. Music producers, journalists, and previous winners cast votes for the nominees, and the results are presented in a spectacular TV show. The spot was constructed to show the glamorous, funny, funky, and exciting moments of the event. The five main categories (pop, laiko, endechno, alternative, and generic) are presented by "virtual" animated stars, performing their acts on different stages. The scenarios, animated in stop-motion, are close

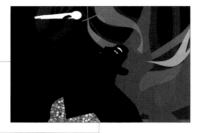

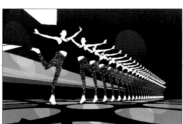

to the aesthetics of music videos. The look is illustrative, fresh, and contemporary.

To save production time, the Velvet creative team filmed many sequences on DV cam. From the DV material, they developed the storyboard and edited it into an animatic, which was then set to music. After client approval, the first part of the animation was done over the filmed sequences. All the frames then had to be reworked by hand because the "stars" are all heavily stylized characters. When the character animations were done, all the backgrounds were animated. The final compositing was done in Flame. Additional graphics were made in 4D and with After Effects.

TOOLS
Adobe After Effects, Adobe Illustrator, Autodesk Flame, Avid Media Composer, Maxon Cinema 4D

CREDITS
Directors: Matthias Zentner, Andrea Bednarz
Producer: Anne Tyroller
Animation: Wiebke Pforr, Maria Regenspurger, Monika Rohner, Alissa Burkel

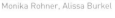

WORLD LEADERS ENTERTAINMENT
USA
TITLE: MIGRATION NATION
CLIENT: SULAKE CORPORATION
FORMAT: DVD CARTOON

PROFILE

World Leaders Entertainment traces its foundation to January 2001, when seven Walt Disney animators and directors jumped ship to form Noodlesoup Productions. Gradually, Noodlesoup added creative, technical, and corporate staff, and rebranded itself as World Leaders Entertainment, which better fitted its expanding presence in the animation industry and its cutting-edge style. The studio now employs a full-time staff of twenty-five. Founded on creative expression, World Leaders specializes in animation that entertains its audiences with whimsy and passion in a spectrum of styles. The studio's directors, designers, programmers, and animators create and produce TV series, commercials, viral content, and web applications.

STEPS TO PRODUCTION

Sulake Corporation came to World Leaders with a well-defined concept for a cartoon; it had elaborate character descriptions and a detailed map of Snout

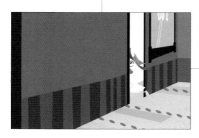

Hill, home town of the online virtual world for young teens, Habbo. From there, Mike Foran, one of the studio's creative directors, wrote the script, designed the main characters, and supervised and directed design, storyboards, audio, and animation.

When developing the film, Foran wanted to concentrate the fun, anything-can-happen, pop-art video-game feel that the online virtual world conveys. He tried to keep the story light and fun, with quirky dialogue and snappy characters. Early in the development process, he decided

he wanted a song to accompany the cartoon. Habbo.com, being populated by real people, is both cute and edgy, so Mike wanted the cartoon to have the same appeal.

Characters and backgrounds were all designed with Macromedia Flash. Next, the storyboards were drafted traditionally on paper. They were then scanned and an animatic was created with in-house scratch audio, using Flash. Using the animatic as a guide, the characters were then fully animated, again using Flash. Once completed, the piece was sent to the

postfacility/sound studio, where music and voice were added, and any last edits were done. Finally, all the elements were brought together and composited in Adobe After Effects.

TOOLS
Adobe After Effects, Apple Final Cut Pro, Macromedia Flash, pencil and paper

CREDITS
Director/Writer: Mike Foran
Producer: Alexandra Otero
Supervising Producer: Jeremy Rosenberg

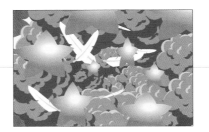

11

MAYA YONESHO
JAPAN
TITLE: UKS UKS
CLIENT: PERSONAL PROJECT
FORMAT: SHORT FILM

PROFILE

Maya Yonesho was born in Japan. In 1998, she received her masters degree in conceptual art and animation, based on traditional Japanese paintings, from Kyoto City University of Arts. Since 1997, she has been making abstract animation synchronized with language, sounds, and music, under the theme "we can understand each other without understanding each other's language." Her films are made up of images from her daily life, as well as things collected while exploring other cultures.

Yonesho lives in Japan but often makes her films abroad: *Introspection* was made in the UK, *Wiener Wuast* in Austria, and *Uks Uks* in Estonia.

STEPS TO CREATION

Yonesho uses her interest in early Japanese art to create images of beauty and simplicity that are based on direct observation of life and on soundtracks that she makes herself. Her soundtracks are constructed from sounds that she has collected and from

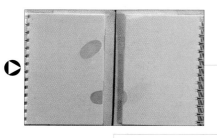   

 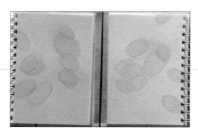  

 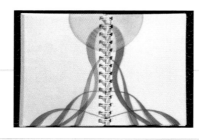  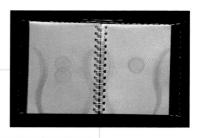

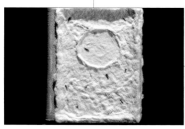 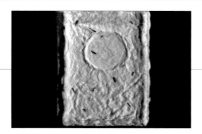 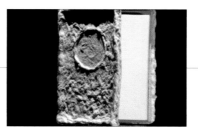 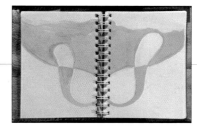

music she made either by herself or with other musicians. Her goal is to give expression to feelings that cannot be adequately expressed in words.

The special quality of Yonesho's work is the subtle changes in texture and feel as the images shift to the soundtrack.

Yonesho started *Uks Uks* as she starts all her films. First, she identified the subject matter in ordinary life that had some special emotional significance for her: her feelings at particular moments in her life, such as when she is with her mother, with friends, or enjoying art. She prepared sounds, voices, and music around the topic, then edited all the sounds into a soundtrack and analyzed the timing to see how many animated drawings she would need.

The drawings were done with ink on paper in spiral-bound notebooks, and then captured using either a traditional 35-mm film camera or a digital camera, for additional processing. This technique is referred to in the film by the recurring use of spiral-bound notebooks. These elaborate on the notion that ideas can be written down, read again, reconfigured, and reborn with new meaning.

In *Uks Uks*, Yonesho worked with eight Estonian bookbinding artists, who made beautiful book covers especially for the film.

TOOLS
Adobe Premiere, Apple Final Cut Pro, pen and paper

CREDITS
Director/Producer/Animation: Maya Yonesho
Camera Operator/Editor: Urmas Joemees
Music/Sound: Sven Grünberg

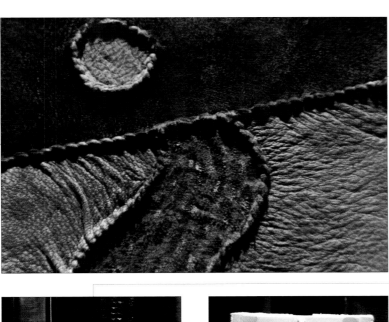
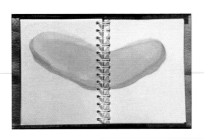

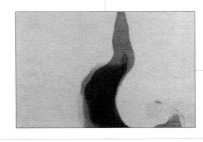

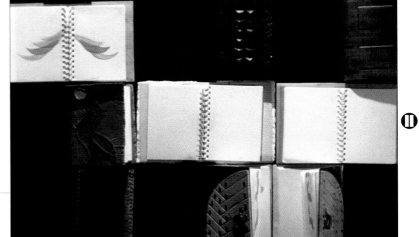
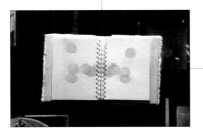
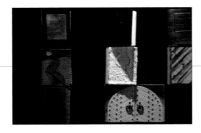

ANASTASIA ZHURAVLEVA
RUSSIA
TITLE: CAUTION! THE DOORS ARE OPENING!
CLIENT: PERSONAL PROJECT
FORMAT: SHORT FILM

PROFILE

Anastasia Zhuravleva was born in 1976 in Obninsk, in Russia's Kaluga province. As a child, she studied ballet, music, dance, drawing, rhythmic gymnastics, and needlework. She graduated from Dubravushka, a humanities high school, in 1994, and went on to study history and philology at the Russian State University for the Humanities in Moscow. She majored in Jewish Studies, and received her degree in 1999. Her thesis, "An Analysis of the Formation of Ethnic Identity amongst Ancient Jews on the Basis of the Tanakh," earned a certificate from the New York Theological Seminary. Zhuravleva also took animation courses, after which she worked as an inbetweener. After a spell as a journalist for a Jewish website, she enrolled in the animation director program of Shar Studio School in Moscow, where, in 2006, she completed her senior film, *Caution! The Doors Are Opening!* It won the award for best debut film at the Open Russian Festival of Animated Film in Suzdal, and first prize for animation at the St. Anna Festival of Debut and Student Films.

At the time of writing, Zhuravleva is working as an animator at the Pilot Studio on the *Gora Samotvetov* (The Mountain of Treasures) project, for which a large collection of traditional Russian folktales and other stories about the peoples of Russia will be animated.

STEPS TO CREATION

Zhuravleva had wanted to make a film about the Moscow Metro ever since she'd arrived in the city. The buttons were inspired by another story she wanted to develop, in which a beggar pretends to be blind, and a little boy throws him a button instead of a coin. The two interwoven stories became the theme for her film.

While drawing the storyboards, Zhuravleva decided she would make a stop-frame film, moving and photographing actual buttons instead of drawing "crowds of them." "I was lucky to become acquainted with a great button collector," she said, "who gifted me a lot of her buttons." Once the storyboards were firmed up, she timed everything out to work out the exact length of each scene and episode. It then took two months to design and create all the props, and the actual filming took five months, with the help of three animators and one operator. Because the storyboards had been so tightly worked out, postproduction took only a month and a half. At this stage the composer scored the music and the sound producer laid in the soundtrack.

The five-minute film was dedicated to all the buttons lost in the Metro.

TOOLS
Adobe Photoshop, Adobe Premiere

CREDITS
Director/Writer/Artwork: Anastasia Zhuravleva
Producer: Sergei Mirzaev
Cinematography: Valentin Sveshnikov
Animation: Tatiana Molodova, Vladimir Kadukhin, Konstantin Romanenko, Anastasia Zhuravleva
Music Composition: Vitalii Basilevskii
Sound: Sofia Trifonova

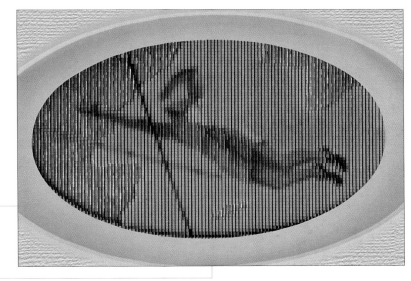

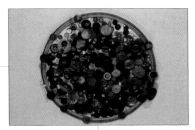
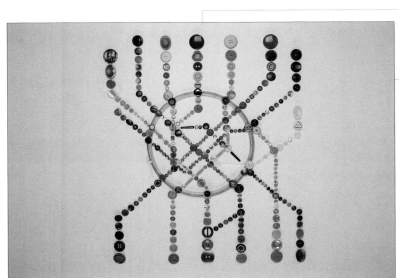

TO ALL THE BUTTONS LOST IN THE METRO

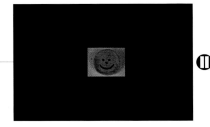

DIRECTORY

5-x-b 5-x-b.com
180 Amsterdam 180amsterdam.com
Absolute Post Production absolutepost.co.uk
Addikt addikt.nl
Adolescent adolescent.tv
Filipe Alçada bermudashorts.com
Arthur Cox worldofarthurcox.co.uk
Augenblick Studios augenblickstudios.com
Liron Bar-akiva lironba@gmail.com
Bl:nd blind.com
Buck buckla.com
CA-Square ca-square.com
Jennifer A. Cable jenniferalayne@gmail.com
Chaotic Unicorn chaoticunicorn.com
Sylvain Chomet djangofilms.co.uk
Rastko Ćirić rastkociric.com
Click 3x click3x.com
Curious Pictures curiouspictures.com
Dancing Diablo Studio dancingdiablo.com
Digital Kitchen d-kitchen.com
Jordie Doubt doubtanimation.ch
EyeballNYC eyeballnyc.com
FilmTecknarna filmtecknarna.se
Lorenzo Fonda cerberoleso.it
Foreign Office foreignoffice.com
Freestyle Collective freestylecollective.com
Fuel fuelvfx.com
Funny Garbage funnygarbage.com
Sophie Gateau sofigato.com

Daryl Graham daryllwgraham@hotmail.com
The Groop thegroop.net
Özgül Gürbüz ozgulgurbuz.deviantart.com
Klara Hajkova strom-animation.cz
Andreas Hykade hykade.de
Murray John bermudashorts.com
Igor Kovalyov igorkovalyov.com
Loyalkaspar loyalkaspar.com
Takagi Masakatsu takagimasakatsu.com
MK12 mk12.com
Motion Theory motiontheory.com
The Moving Picture Company moving-picture.com
Nailgun* nailgun.tv
Odeon odeon.com.pl
PanOptic panoptic.org
Janet Perlman janetperlman.com
Fons Schiedon fonztv.nl
J.J. Sedelmaier Productions jjsedelmaier.com
Shilo shilodesign.co.uk
Alexandre Siqueira alexandresiqueira.blogspot.com
Studio aka studioaka.co.uk
Arthur Suydam arthursuydam.com
Tak Productions West tak77@sbcglobal.net
Tandem Films tandemfilms.com
Velvet Mediendesign velvet.de
World Leaders Entertainment worldleadersentertainment.com
Maya Yonesho http://homepage3.nifty.com/maya_y/
Anastasia Zhuravleva avzhuravleva@yahoo.ru

For information on the technical terms used in this book, please refer to: highend3d.com/dictionary

PICTURE CREDITS

The illustrations in this book have been reproduced courtesy of the artists and the following organizations:

pp. 4 (inset), 120–21: Touch and Go Records; pp. 6 (insets), 99, 150–51: MTV; pp. 9 (insets), 56–57: Winterthur; pp. 12–13: Ecko Unlimited; pp. 14–15: BET J; pp. 16–17, 176: Adidas International; pp. 18–19: Vodafone; pp. 20–21: XS4ALL; pp. 22–23: CMT; pp. 24–25: TMF UK; pp. 28–29: Kellogg's; pp. 30–35, 78, 79: Comedy Central; pp. 38–39: MTV2; pp. 40–41: Specialized; pp. 42–43: Cingular Wireless; pp. 44–45: G4 Media, Inc.; pp. 46–47: VH1 (New York); pp. 50–51, 54–55: Nicktoons; pp. 52–53: JVC Jazz Festival; pp. 58–59: Ministry of Culture, Belgrade; pp. 60–61: Jive Records; pp. 62–63: Samsung; pp. 64–65: Toyota Mexico; pp. 66–67: Volkswagen; pp. 68–69: Sesame Workshop; pp. 70–71, 92–93: JetBlue; pp. 72–73: Sundance; pp. 74–75: Coca-

Cola; pp. 82–83: Independent Film Festival of Boston; pp. 84–85: Sundek/ J. Walter Thompson; pp. 86–87: The Weinstein Company/Pathé Pictures/ BBC Films; pp. 88–89: Nickelodeon; pp. 90–91, 152–53: Fuel TV; pp. 96–97: Fox/A&E; p. 98: Disney; pp. 100–101: Cartoon Network; pp. 102–103: Fascineshion.com; pp. 104–105: Nabisco; pp. 106–107: Aiwa; pp. 110–111: Zlin Film College; p. 116: Island Records; p. 117: BBC; pp. 122–23: Sampo Bank; pp. 128–29: Hewlett-Packard; pp. 130–31: Reebok International; pp. 132–33: Channel 4; p. 134: Spike TV; p. 135: Indemand Networks; pp. 136–39: Odeon Rybarczyk Productions; pp. 140–41: Scion; pp. 142–43: National Film Board of Canada; pp. 144–45: MTV Asia;

pp. 146–47: MTV Asia/Motorola; pp. 148–49: Submarine Channel; pp. 154–55: Toyota Motor Sales USA/Scion; pp. 156–57: ICAM; pp. 158–59: Camelot; pp. 160–61: Paranoid Delusions; pp. 162–63: History Channel; pp. 164–65: BBC Two; pp. 166–67: Mega Channel, Greece; pp. 168–69: Sulake Corporation; pp. 174–75: Adidas International

Every effort has been made to trace and contact copyright holders of the illustrations reproduced in this book. The publisher will be happy to correct in subsequent editions any errors or omissions that are brought to its attention.

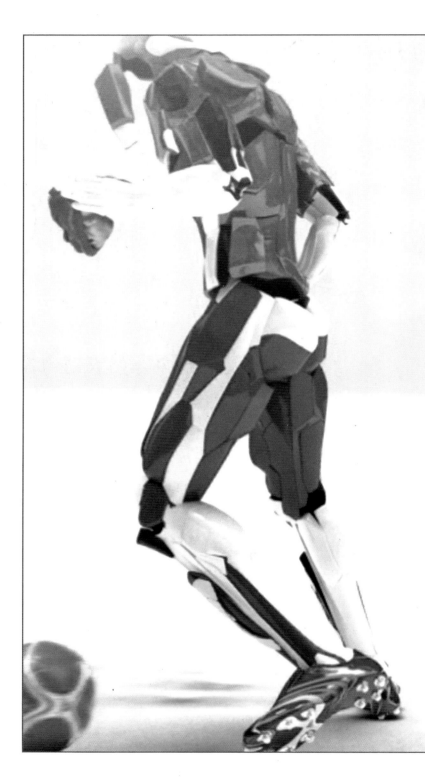

Dedicated to all animators around the world.

Judith and Spencer thank Joan Brookbank, Elizabeth Choi, Hugh Merrell, Nicola Bailey, Claire Chandler, and everyone at Merrell Publishers. Very special thanks to J.J. Sedelmaier, Reeves Lehman, Howard Beckerman, Chris Robinson, David Levy, Nancy Phelps, and Kayak Bob, who saved the day.

A huge thank-you to all the companies and individual animators who contributed their talents. Extra-special thanks to those who saw us through and gave us inspiration: Ned Davis, Karen Karibian, and all the classic animation we grew up with and still enjoy!

First published 2007 by
Merrell Publishers Limited

Head office
81 Southwark Street
London SE1 0HX

New York office
740 Broadway, Suite 1202
New York, NY 10003

merrellpublishers.com

Text copyright © 2007 Spencer Drate
   and Judith Salavetz
Design and layout copyright © 2007
   Spencer Drate and Judith Salavetz
Illustrations copyright © the copyright
   holders; see p. 175

British Library Cataloguing-in-Publication data:
Drate, Spencer
Pure animation : steps to creation with 57 cutting-edge animators
1. Animation (Cinematography)
I. Title II. Salavetz, Jutka
778.5'347

ISBN-13: 978-1-8589-4365-7
ISBN-10: 1-8589-4365-5

Produced by Merrell Publishers Limited
Art Direction and Design:
   Judith Salavetz and Spencer Drate
Technical Writer: Robert Huszar
Copy-edited by Diane Pengelly
Proof-read by Elizabeth Tatham

Printed and bound in China

Cover design: Judith Salavetz,
   Spencer Drate with Jeremy Miller
Interior design: Judith Salavetz with
   additional design by Jeremy Miller

Cover, front (top to bottom):
5-x-b, *Wick'd*, see p. 14; Shilo, *Imagine This*, see p. 152; J.J. Sedelmaier Productions, *Look What You've Done*, see p. 150; Studio aka, *The Big Win*, see p. 158
Cover, back (top to bottom):
Foreign Office, *Nickelodeon Crunch*, see p. 88; Takagi Masakatsu, *Light Pool*, see p. 124; Click 3x, *Bom Bom Bom*, see p. 60; Sylvain Chomet/th1ng, *Tomorrow*, see p. 56

p. 1: Foreign Office • *MTV Load*
pp. 2–3, 4–5, 8–9, 10–11: Andreas Hykade • *The Runt*, see p. 114
p. 4 (inset): Loyalkaspar • *Fortress*, see p. 120
pp. 6–7: Image by Manabu Inada
p. 6 (insets): J.J. Sedelmaier Productions • *Look What You've Done*, see p. 150
p. 9 (insets): Sylvain Chomet • *Tomorrow*, see p. 56
pp. 174–75: 180 Amsterdam • *Adstar*
This page: 180 Amsterdam • *Modular Man*, see p. 16